CREATIVE
STITCHED
SHIBORI

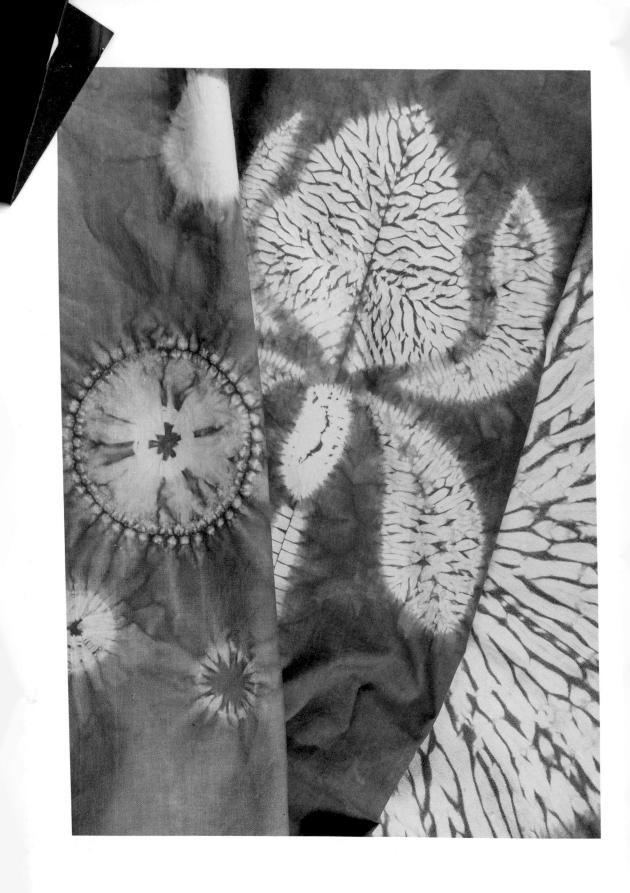

CREATIVE
STITCHED
SHIBORI

Annabel Wilson

THE CROWOOD PRESS

CONTENTS

INTRODUCTION

Discovering shibori has been a life-changing moment for me. What fascinated me from the very beginning was the simplicity of the practice of stitched shibori.

I enjoy the uncomplicated routine of taking a plain piece of fabric and by stitching into the warp and weft of the textile I can produce something personal and fresh. It may be a geometric pattern or take the form of an object from nature. The finished dyed designs may look very complicated, but they are all created following straightforward steps and using basic stitches.

Stitched shibori is just variations on running stitch and oversew stitch. Just follow the markings you have made on the fabric. Nothing can be simpler. And then by adding elements of binding the cloth in a disciplined manner, a multitude of designs can be made.

Stitched shibori practice does need forward planning and thinking through the steps and the order of those steps to achieve the design you want. It is in this way that it differs from tie-dye. Tie-dye is a random approach to making markings on fabric. The designs made with tie-dye are generally hit-or-miss.

Another difference beween tie-dye and stitched shibori is that shibori is a slower and more meditative means to realise a pattern on fabric. It is the mindful practice of needle and thread through fabric, following a line of marks that, after dyeing, will form a beautiful design individual to you. Even if you follow a pattern, your shibori will still be personal to you. Your stitching is like handwriting; the colour of dye you choose; the particular effect of the dye through the fabric and stitch. All these diverse elements will lead to an authentic and singular result.

HOW TO USE THIS BOOK

Each chapter will introduce you to a stitched shibori technique, starting with the simplest and most straightforward. Gradually, your skills will build, adding to your competence in shibori. Even with the simplest of stitches, wonderful designs can be created. And you will build on those, step by step. As the chapters progress, we will put the different techniques together to produce more complicated designs. But by following the patterns and planning carefully and thoughtfully, you will find that it is easy to create wonderful and inspiring designs in stitched shibori. I am hoping that picking up this book will open up a whole new world for you to explore and create. A love of hand stitching is all you require.

Pattern templates are not included in the book. To copy a pattern, just take a photograph of the page and print out to the sizes indicated and trace onto your fabric.

I wish you much joy as you explore shibori and discover how to create your own remarkable fabrics.

◀ A collection of stitched shibori fabrics dyed with madder root.

CHAPTER 1

MATERIALS AND EQUIPMENT

We begin our shibori adventure by gathering all the bits and pieces we require. The equipment we need for shibori will be found in most baskets, cabinets, or containers where you keep your general sewing equipment. However, if you are completely new to sewing, the apparatus required is minimal.

The more complicated components to achieve successful shibori results are related to your selection of fabrics and dye stuffs. We will look in detail at how different fabrics affect the results so you can be clear on the best fabrics to use.

Also, we are going to consider different dye options and the effect that has on your creative shibori patterns. The full information on how to use different dyes can be found in comprehensive detail in books only dedicated to the process of dyeing. Consequently, unless you are already a dyer, I will recommend using the simplest dye process possible. This enables you to learn and discover the stitches, and play with the patterns and possibilities of stitched shibori. Dyeing fabrics can be a complicated art to fathom. It is a wonderful adventure in itself, but can be a brake on moving forward in shibori.

Subsequently, once your interest is piqued you can go on to discover and explore the wonderful world of natural dyeing, or delve into the enjoyable process of mixing your own special colours with chemical dyes.

SEWING EQUIPMENT

The requirements are very simple: needles, thread and, of course, some scissors. Let's consider these in turn.

The basic tools for creating shibori, a good selection of needles, strong polyester sewing thread, a small scissors and chopped short lengths of cotton to make tags.

◀ Stitched fabric with some essential shibori tools.

Sewing Thread

The main requirement for sewing shibori is a very strong, nearly unbreakable thread. For all the stitching use standard polyester or nylon sewing thread. Additionally, test the polyester thread by pulling hard to check that it does not break. Some of the cheaper polyester threads break rather too easily. I have tried them as a drive to save money. I recommend Gütermann Sew-All thread. I have used this consistently through all the years I have been sewing shibori and it very rarely breaks.

I suggest choosing a strong and contrasting colour to the white or cream of the fabric. Select a red, dark green or blue, or strong gold. The shibori stitching can appear quite complicated and dense across the fabric, so a contrasting thread helps you stay in control of your sewing.

Needles

I recommend sharps in size 7–10 or embroidery needles in size 4–8. I love the slow process of hand sewing, and consequently I prefer using short needles. However, some shibori sewers prefer a longer needle, which enables them to get more stitches completed on one pass through of the needle. Here there will be a little experimentation to find the needles you are happy with.

Scissors

You will require a small pair of embroidery scissors or snips and a larger pair for cutting the fabrics. The small scissors are very useful for carrying around and sewing your shibori on the go.

Tags

The other principal thread you need to begin your shibori is a double-knit weight cotton or wool thread. It is preferable to select a white or cream thread, just in case there is the possibility of dye from the yarn transferring to the fabric.

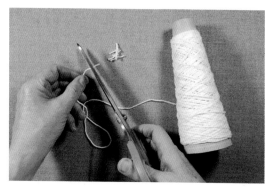

To create the tags used to secure the stitching use double-knit weight cotton thread and cut into 1.5–2.5cm (5/8in–1in) lengths.

This is cut into 1.5–2.5cm (5/8–1in) lengths. You don't have to be exact here! These form the tags that are inserted at the beginning and end of every row of sewing.

Inserting the tags helps greatly at the end of the process of shibori when you are unpicking all those rows of tightly gathered stitches. The tags clearly indicate the ends of the rows and give you something to catch hold of.

MATERIALS FOR BINDING

Binding Thread

Create a selection of assorted strong threads for binding. Different threads have distinctive

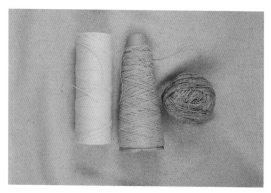

A selection of threads for the binding of the shibori designs: an extremely strong cotton warp, a linen thread and a ball of nettle fibre.

A selection of beads, dowel and cotton reels that are useful to use to bind into the fabric to create a shibori resist.

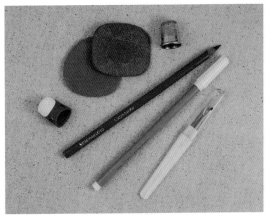

Miscellaneous tools for marking the fabric, to protect the fingers and for the final unpicking of shibori stitching after dyeing.

effects, which we will explore in future chapters. My particular selection includes a terrifically strong weaver's warp thread, like a double-knit weight, a 3-ply/fingering weight linen thread and a nettle fibre.

Beads and Cores

Here is another diverse set of items to put together. As with the threads, begin to gather an assortment of beads and small objects to bind into the fabric.

Collect together tiny decorative glass beads of 2mm ($^1/_{16}$in), through to small wooden beads of 4mm ($^3/_{16}$in) to some larger chunky beads.

In addition, the other kind of objects you need for binding are of a larger diameter and are called cores. These are needed when creating large white circles on the fabric. Examples are items such as old cotton reels or balsa wood dowels of 2.5cm (1in) diameter. The latter are easy to cut and available from model making stores. You can also make your own 'cores' from scrap fabric, which I will show you in Chapter 5.

MISCELLANEOUS TOOLS

There is a small selection of additional bits and pieces that you will need.

Fabric Markers

It is very important to draw your shibori designs on the fabric, to give yourself clear guidance of the lines to follow with your folding and stitching. The more old-fashioned way is to use tailor's chalks, available in various colours in block or pencil format. These do not disappear completely, so select a colour close to your final planned dye colour. The positive aspect to their use is it is more like drawing with a pencil on paper.

Alternatively, use a water-soluble or air-soluble marker to transfer the design. This disappears over time or with water.

Hand Protection

It is helpful to protect your fingers from too many needle jabs. There are now many different kinds of thimble available, which ensures you can find one that is comfortable for you.

When doing lots of sewing the hands get dry and however careful you are, the needles will prick the fingers. It is worth keeping the hands well moisturised, as rough skin constantly snags on the thread and on fine cotton and silk.

Seam Ripper

This is a very necessary tool to use for unpicking all the stitching after dyeing. A small pair of embroidery scissors can be used, but there is more danger of catching the fabric and making a small hole than when using the seam ripper.

WHERE TO DO IT

As shibori stitching is time-consuming, it is a wonderful idea to maximise the time you can use to stitch designs. A very enjoyable part of shibori sewing is that you can stitch anywhere. The amount of equipment needed is minimal. It is very easy to carry all the necessary tools with you.

I have a small basket containing all that is needed for shibori, and I can carry it around the home, allowing me to pick it up as and when I want.

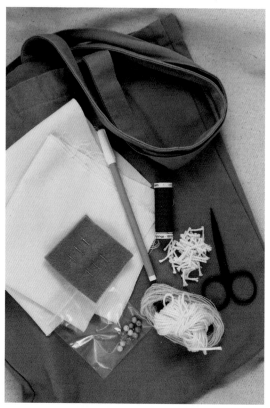

A cotton bag just big enough to hold a selection of equipment to take when travelling so no time is wasted.

A small basket to keep a selection of shibori equipment and fabrics to carry around the house, keeping everything in one place.

When I take a train journey or go away it is a simple matter to take a small cotton bag with all the bits and pieces for stitching. Prepare and draw your designs on the fabric in advance, as that is more difficult to do on the move.

CHOOSING YOUR FABRIC

Shibori can be sewn into many fabrics, but I recommend starting with a nice soft cotton for your first experiments. The cotton fabric needs to be soft but quite tightly woven. If it is a loose weave, the shibori pattern will lose its definition. I suggest a light cotton calico (muslin in the USA) or voile. Some poplin and percale can be too closely woven for ease of working the needle in and out of the fabric.

Silk is a beautiful fabric to use but is difficult to work as it slips and slides. It therefore needs tacking or basting to hold the folded shapes.

Take care if reusing old fabrics such as cotton or linen sheets, because if it is worn the fabric can rip or tear. You are putting the fabric under a lot of stress with the gathering, dyeing and unpicking.

Weight of Fabrics

Many textile suppliers will be able to tell you the weights of their fabrics in grammes per square metre or ounces per square yard. As a guide, a fabric weight of between 2.6oz per sq yd (90g per sq m) and 5oz per sq yd (170g per sq m) is ideal. My favourite fabric is around 3.5oz per sq yd (120g sq m).

Preparation of Fabrics

Many fabrics have a finish on them, which needs to be removed before use, so that the dye adheres to the fabric. The process is called scouring. Wash the textiles at 60°C (140°F) before you start, to ensure that any finish is removed using washing soda or detergent, in a machine or by hand. To avoid the need for doing this, find fabrics described as prepared for dyeing (PFD).

Shibori Results on Different Fabrics

Various weights and weaves of fabrics will give varied results. The same dye on different fabrics will give a range of shades and tones. Search for a fabric you like, do some experiments, see how it reacts to dye and the shibori stitching and stick with that. There will always be elements of trial and error in finding the best fabric. Do not set off on a complicated design without being sure of your fabric choice and having done a few samples first.

Each of these fabrics has been dyed with the same colour and concentration of dye. Exactly the same design was drawn on each and stitched in the same way.

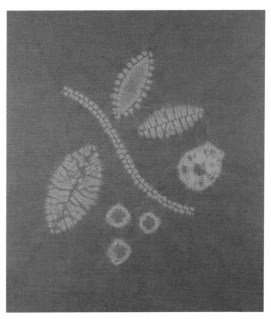

This first sample is a calico, a nice tight weave with a soft handle. The pattern is clear and each type of shibori stitch is sharp. The result is exactly what I would expect from my original design and dyed with a chemical dye.

The second sample here is a cotton hemp mix with a pronounced slub in the weave, a more textured fabric. The pattern is well defined, but the texture makes the fabric more difficult to gather up tightly and the effect is a little grainier.

This third sample is made on a thin muslin with a loose weave. The pattern is distorted because of the weave and the dye seeps in too much and creates a blurred pattern. This fabric sample illustrates the negative effect of using such a fabric.

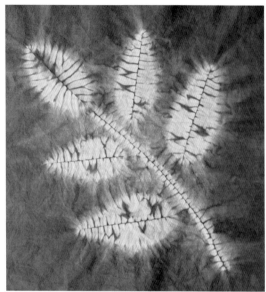

The leaf sprig dyed with indigo. The resist is whiter compared with the next two. Additionally, the individual lines of stitching within the leaf shapes are not distinct after dyeing. There is a slightly fuzzy effect around the design, almost a halo. Note the paler areas where the leaves meet the stem, a result of not being able to get as much indigo into those areas because of the gathering.

ADVICE ON DYES

The final ingredient to make the shibori come alive is the dye process. Here we will consider the various dyeing options available. If you already do fibre-reactive dyeing or indigo or plant dyeing, you will just need to be aware of the slightly different effects these dyes will have on your finished designs. We cannot achieve exactly the same results with chemical dyes as with using indigo. Indigo has traditionally been used for shibori and it does give a very distinctive effect.

The Effects of Individual Dyes

I have dyed exactly the same sprig design with different dyes and immediately you can see the particular effects of each dye. There will be subtle differences depending on the fabric used. All my comments and suggestions about the effects of dye are based on the visual

This is a heavy weight silk fabric. Note how different the colour is on silk. Silk is a slippery customer to sew shibori. Note that the larger leaf at the bottom right is angled differently from the other three designs. It is a challenge to keep to the drawn pattern with silk.

The leaf sprig in gold, dyed with fibre-reactive dyes. The first major contrast is how distinctive the lines of stitching in the leaves remain after dyeing. Also, the outlines are crisper, and there is no halo around the leaf shapes. Though there is a slight paler area of dyeing around the top two leaves and the stem, it is a lot less marked than in indigo. Chemical dyes penetrate the fabric more readily and when using darker chemical dyes, the areas of stitch resist will often have a hint of the dye colour, not a complete white resist.

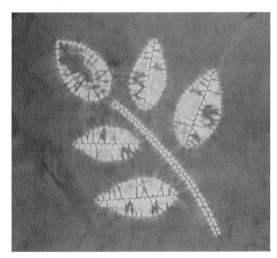

The same design dyed with natural madder root has subtle differences to the other two. Again, the outline is crisper, and the stitch line is more apparent. But the resist is sharper and whiter, as the plant dyes produce a clearer resist. Due to the necessary process of preparing the fabric prior to dyeing, there is sometimes a little mottling or unevenness in the background colour. That can be considered all part of the magic of using plant dyes.

effects I have seen or achieved over many years of practice.

The conclusion is that all dye types can give you great results. But to understand the subtle differences that occur will help you not feel disappointment when you see a design in indigo, and then dye with fibre-reactive dyes that do not achieve exactly the same result.

Colour Selection

Furthermore, it is important to carefully consider the colours to use. You can see throughout the book an avoidance of soft pastel and pale colours such as yellow, pale pinks and aqua. After all that detailed stitching and careful hand sewing taking many hours, you want a good contrast between the original fabric and the dye, allowing your design to shine out.

Information on Different Dye Methods

We will consider the varied selection of dyes available to you. I have used all the dyes I am recommending here. If you are completely new to craft dyeing, I would suggest using the simplest method to enable you to start right in with creating with shibori. As we will be dyeing small pieces of fabric, methods of weighing out small amounts of dye are essential.

A selection of chemical dyes: Rit, Dylon and Procion (fibre-reactive) dye powder, with different measures to accurately weigh the dyestuff.

A bottle of prepared indigo stock, dark, mysterious and messy, ready to be added to the vat.

A collection of natural plant dye materials. With plant dyes, a thermometer is an important piece of equipment. Clockwise from bottom left: alkanet, weld, rhubarb root, madder root, onlon skins.

With all these methods I talk about there is detailed information available on product websites, videos online and in the many books written on the subject.

Firstly, chemical dyes include brands such as Dylon, Rit and fibre-reactive dyes. The quickest method is to use a liquid dye such as Rit. I use this dye type to test my designs, as it is simple to use and easy to measure out small amounts of dye for small fabric pieces. Fibre-reactive dyes are a little more complex to use, requiring salt and soda ash to be added in measured quantities. The colours are very concentrated and potent, as well as having an endless range of shades. It is essential to wear a face mask when dealing with the powdered dye.

Indigo dyeing and creating a vat is a fascinating adventure. It is a messy process, and the vat preferably needs making outside or in a garage or shed. The alchemy of indigo dyeing is quite magical, and it is astonishing to see the blue colour develop as the fabric meets the air. The best way to learn how to dye with indigo is to join a workshop and learn from an experienced indigo dyer. Once you have successfully made an indigo vat, it is easy to repeat with confidence.

There is a wonderful world to explore when deciding to use natural dyes. The procedure is lengthier because fabrics need preparing to receive the dye, a technique called mordanting. Many fabrics can be mordanted together and you can store them for use as needed. Natural dyes can either be purchased from specialist suppliers or collected from the wild or your garden. The particular wonder of the practice of natural plant dyeing is how the colours go together. There is a gentleness to the tones, which complement each other.

Equipment For Dyeing

Each method of dyeing has slightly different requirements. With all dyeing it is imperative that the equipment used for dyeing is kept solely for that purpose. Any specialist book on dyeing methods will have a comprehensive list of all the tools and pans you will need.

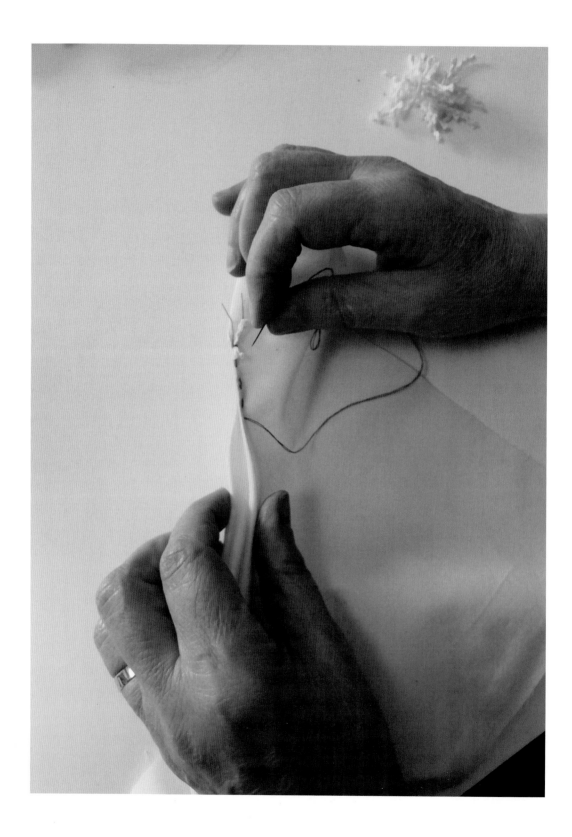

CHAPTER 2

GETTING STARTED: THE BASICS

This chapter will outline all the little tricks and secrets to help you with your shibori stitching. If you can learn these basic steps, all that follows will be much easier to grasp.

There are tips for transferring your design to the fabric. It is always a good idea to sketch the design on a piece of paper first, enabling any rubbing out and alteration before attempting to transfer the pattern to the fabric.

We will consider how to start and finish a row to ensure the thread does not slip through the fabric. It is essential when gathering the stitching that the thread holds fast. If stitching becomes loose, the pattern will be lost or parts of it will be faint. This will produce a disappointing result.

It is also important to ensure all the stitching is pulled up, right back to the beginning of the row. There are some useful hints on how to achieve this.

There is also information on joining threads if you are sewing a larger piece of work, plus guidance on how to sew with two needles from one point. This is helpful if sewing a form that incorporates a sharp angle in the stitch outline.

TRANSFER YOUR DESIGN TO THE FABRIC

Sketch and play about with elements of the pattern you want to create with pencil on paper. Once you are pleased with your design, draw over the outlines with a dark felt tip pen. This will ensure that you can see your pattern through the fabric. In nearly all cases, you will be able to glimpse the design through the fabric if you have chosen the right weight of fabric. Occasionally, if you are using a heavier fabric such as a linen, you may need to tape the pattern to a window and use natural light to help see through the fabric, or use a light box if you have one.

Attach the paper pattern to the table with tape. Likewise, hold the fabric firmly in place with further pieces of tape. Use a water or air soluble marker or tailor's chalk to carefully trace the design on to the fabric. Then you are ready to start sewing.

◀ The mindful sewing of shibori patterns, one simple stitch at a time.

After you have firmed up your shibori design, draw over the pencil drawing with a dark felt tip. Making a strong dark line ensures the drawing can be seen through the fabric. Tape the pattern drawing to the table.

Lay the fabric over the drawing. In nearly all cases, if you have chosen the right weight of fabric, you will be able to glimpse the design through the fabric. You can also fix the drawing to a window and use natural light to help you see clearly.

Tape the fabric to the table to hold it firmly on top of the drawing. This ensures it doesn't slip while you transfer the drawing onto the fabric.

Using a water- or air-soluble marker, start drawing the outline of your pattern on to the fabric from the drawing beneath. Follow your lines and markings as accurately as possible.

It is helpful to copy all the markings, including where you will fold the fabric and a little stop at the end of a long line, such as the leaf and the stem here.

The drawing is transferred to the fabric. Double check that you have copied all the lines. You are then ready to start the shibori sewing.

HOW TO STITCH

How To Start a Row of Shibori Stitching

All shibori stitching is carried out with the thread doubled. There are no exceptions to this. This is for a number of reasons; strength of your sewing thread – if one thread should break you have another left that you can stitch in – and for ease of finishing off each row, as will be clear in the next section.

Starting with your double thread, tie a small cotton or wool tag at the very end of the double thread. The tag ensures that your thread does not pull through the fabric. The tag is fixed in place by creating a looped knot, left thread over right, place the little tag in and pull tight. Next tie another knot on top of the first, right thread over left, and pull to make sure the tag is secure. You are ready to start a row of stitches.

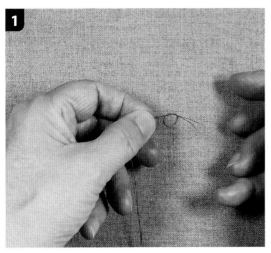

Always use the thread double. Create a loop in the end of the double thread, taking left over right, and holding the thread steady.

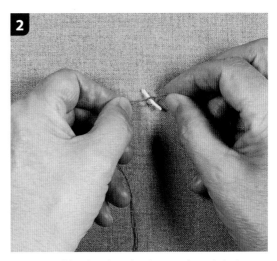

Insert one of the short lengths of cotton through the loop, you will speed up over time with this process. Pull the thread tightly to create a knot to firmly hold the cotton tag.

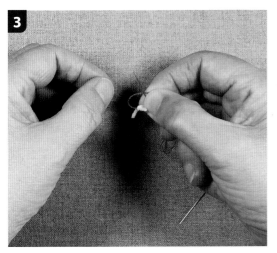

To ensure the tag stays firmly attached, make a second loop, this time right over left.

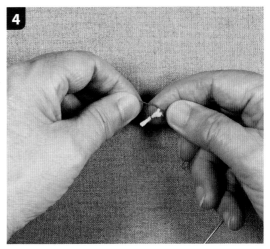

Complete the loop, thereby creating a strong reef knot. The tag will be securely held.

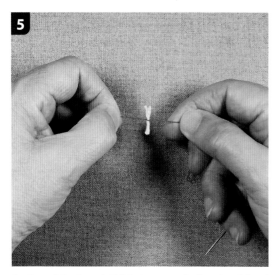

5

Again, pull the threads tightly to ensure the knot is solid and the tag is fixed in place.

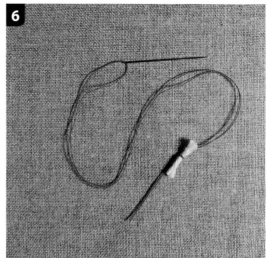

6

Needle, thread, with the tag held in place, all ready to begin sewing your first rows of stitched shibori.

How To Finish a Row of Shibori Stitching

Once the row is complete, firstly trim the thread to a manageable length of about 7cm (2¾in). Pull up the threads, ensuring that the gathers are distributed evenly. Separate the two sewing threads and place a tag between

them. Then tie this in place with a reef knot. First, pass the right thread over the left and make a loop, pulling the threads tight. Following this, make a second loop, the left thread over the right this time. This secures the reef knot. I sometimes add another knot just to be sure.

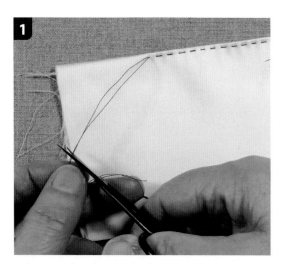

1

A short row of stitching has been completed and we are ready to gather and secure the row. Always trim the length of surplus cotton to a manageable length of around 7cm (2¾in).

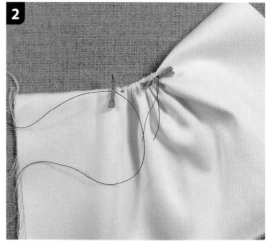

2

Gather the fabric by pulling the stitches using both strands of thread. Separate the two threads and place a tag between them.

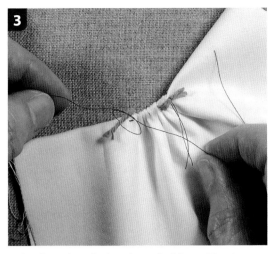

Make a loop, the right thread over the left, catching the tag.

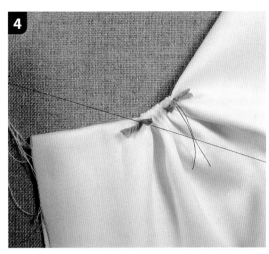

Next, secure the tag firmly by pulling the threads tight.

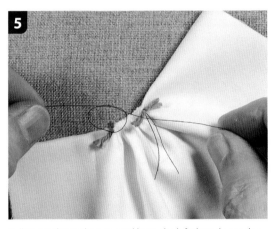

Following this make a second loop, the left thread over the right this time. This makes a reef knot.

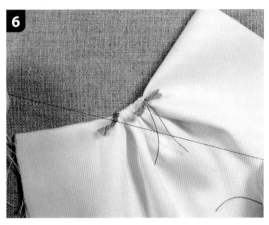

Again, pull the threads away from each other to secure the tag and therefore the row of stitches.

Stitch Length and Spacing

For the majority of patterns, the optimum distance of stitching is 2mm ($^1/_{16}$in) away from the fold, through both layers of fabric. Maintain this regular distance away from the fold, unless your design calls for a tapered line. This is also something you can experiment with and find different effects by changing the distance from the fold.

The stitch length can vary, but approximately 3mm ($^1/_8$in) long will give you a neat, regular pattern. You can experiment with varying the length of stitch and note what effect this has.

With thicker fabrics the stitch length will be longer and with a larger space between stitches. It will also be necessary to stitch a little further away from the fold.

When stitching multiple rows of parallel stitching, either through just one layer of fabric (mokume shibori) or through two layers (miru shibori) the stitches need to vary in length, between 3–6mm (1/8–1/4in). These stitches must also be staggered to achieve the wonderful randomness of these designs.

Rows are placed between 5–8 mm (3/16–5/16in) apart, dependent on the fabric weight. An ideal distance on most fabric is 6mm (1/4in).

When using running stitches through a fold, the stitching is 2mm (1/16in) away from the fold.

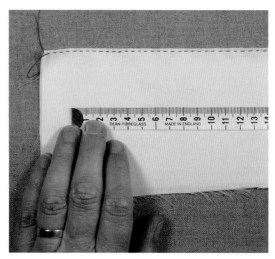

Stitch length can vary, but approximately 3mm (1/8in) long will give you a neat, regular pattern.

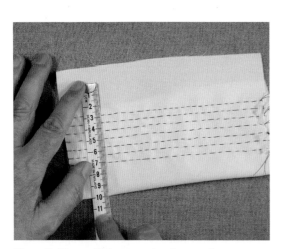

When stitching multiple rows, as in miru or mokume shibori, 6–8mm (1/4in–5/16in) is a good distance to allow between rows.

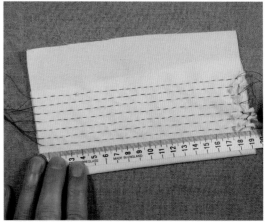

With multiple rows the stitching needs to be staggered. Also, each length of stitch is varied, between 3 to 6mm (1/8in–1/4in) long.

ADDITIONAL HELPFUL HINTS

Gathering Multiple Rows

When pulling up a number of parallel rows of stitching, it is most important to be sure that all the rows are pulled up equally, and to ensure they are gathered back to the very beginning of each row. Arrange all the threads in your hand, grip and gather them together. In this way you will make certain that you are pulling all threads equally. Also, look carefully at each row to make sure they are fully gathered. This attention to detail at this point ensures a good result. Next, row by row give a final pull and tie a tag into the end of each row of stitches. Work methodically down the fabric to be certain that you do not miss a row.

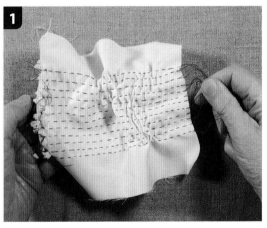

When gathering multiple threads, it is good practice to hold all the thread ends and pull them up together, easing the fabric firmly but gently back to the beginning of each row.

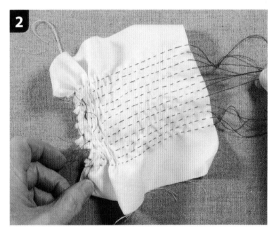

By pulling the stitches up all together, it ensures that each and every row is gathered fully back to the start. If all the stitches are not fully gathered it spoils the pattern overall.

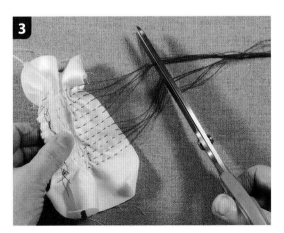

The threads after pulling up will be very long. Trim them back to 7cm (2¾in); the threads are then much easier to handle.

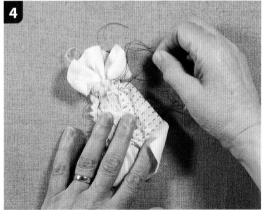

Next, row by row give a final pull, separate the two threads, and tie a tag into the end of each row of stitches. Work methodically down the fabric to be certain that you do not miss a row.

Working on Complicated Patterns

Working on a shibori design containing many different elements has its challenges. Where rows of stitching and pattern are close together, it is most helpful to use two contrasting thread colours for the stitching. Using two colours makes sure you are less likely to miss a short row of stitching hidden right next to complicated multiple rows.

Joining Threads

When you become more adventurous and start making larger scale designs in shibori, you may well need to join your threads, as it is not possible to complete the whole length with one thread. There is a technique to do this as you need to be absolutely certain that the second thread does not catch the last stitch of the starting row.

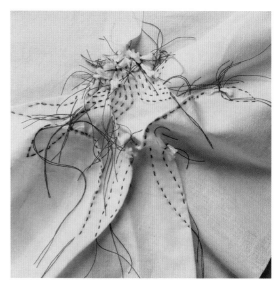

A complicated shibori design where contrasting thread colours of red and green are used to help with clarity and ensure when gathering all the rows of stitches are gathered.

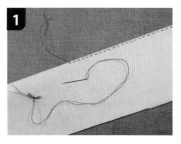

Joining a new thread halfway along the work is a simple procedure. Leave the tail of the first length of stitching free.

Thread your needle again and attach a tag. Enter the needle with the new thread at the end of the last visible stitch.

Bring the needle out right next to the free ends of the last row, making certain that the second thread does not catch the last stitch of the starting row.

To be absolutely sure that the first length of thread is free and can be gathered, give a tug on the free ends to ensure you have not caught the last stitch with the new thread.

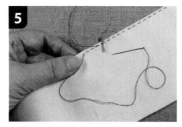

Once you have checked that the previous thread is free you can continue your stitching of the row.

Enter the needle with the new thread at the end of the last visible stitch and bring the needle out right next to the free ends of the last row. Then give a tug on the free ends to ensure you have not caught the last stitch with the new thread.

Stitching with Two Needles from One Point

This is a most helpful technique if a form you want to create has a sharp angle. It can be used to make leaf or petal shapes that result in a similar texture to miru shibori. With further distance between each row of stitching lines, the lines of stitching become visible, providing another design possibility.

This method can be used through a single layer, but has applications for designs through two layers. An example of this is sewing a diamond in miru shibori. A better result is achieved if the stitching is started at the point of the diamond with two needles.

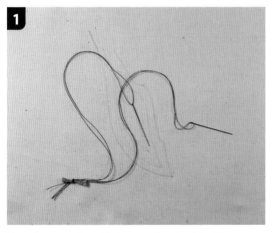

Thread two needles with the same length of double thread. Tie the tag in the end of all four threads, ready to start sewing.

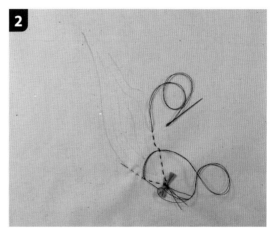

One needle is entered, and the row of stitching begun. Take the other needle in the other direction and follow the outline.

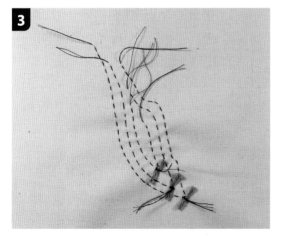

The stitching complete, with new double threads and needles starting from the sharply angled point.

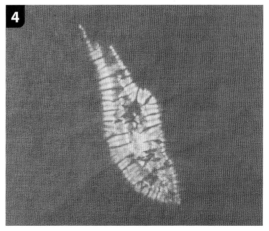

The completed and dyed result of using two needles. Diverse effects can be achieved by spacing the lines further apart.

CHAPTER 3

ORI-NUI AND MAKI-NUI SHIBORI

We start our discovery of stitched shibori with an in-depth look at ori-nui shibori. I see this stitch as an essential building block in creating and designing with shibori. Though it is one of the most straightforward stitches you can learn, you will discover it has many variations and possibilities. By subtly altering and manipulating the line of your stitching, you are able to produce an astonishing range of patterns.

It is so simple to execute, and you will be amazed by the variations that are possible. The ori-nui pattern is formed by making a plain row of running stitches. These stitches are sewn close to the fold through two layers of fabric. This builds a clear, crisp line.

We will also explore a variation on ori-nui, called maki-nui, which is a kind of oversew stitch and produces a rather pleasing chevron stripe.

In this chapter I will show you how, by effortlessly tapering the line of stitching or taking your line of stitches away from the fold, a multitude of designs can be built. Also, using the stitch in multiple clusters and compositions promises further potential for creativity. It can be used to create a bunch of flowers, fronds of grass, a track in a landscape, leaves on a twig, an outline for petals or a leaf, from simple to complex, depending on your skills and dexterity.

You will discover your own variations and arrangements over time.

In my first days of playing and devising patterns in shibori, I used just this easy stitch along with just two others and discovered myriad ideas with limitless potential.

First, I am going to show you the basic stitch and what pattern that produces on the fabric.

Equipment Needed for Ori-Nui Shibori Stitch

Collect what you will need for starting work: a piece of cotton fabric 20 × 20cm (8 × 8in) with some polyester thread – choose a good strong colour that you can see easily. You will need a

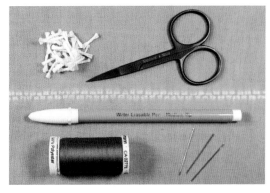

This is what you are aiming for, a finished and dyed line of ori-nui stitch shown alongside the basic tools required for making this stitch.

◀ Dancing leaves, an example of the lovely designs that can be achieved using ori-nui stitch.

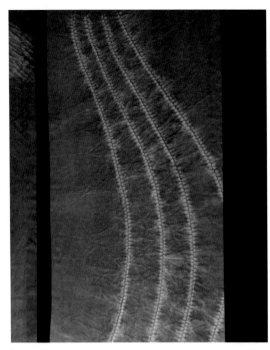

Using just four curved lines of ori-nui shibori, with a varied spacing, it can suggest a track as they flow and widen down the fabric. (Photo: Daniel Rushall)

With multiple straight lines of the stitch very close together, a rhythm is created. Use this to make a pleasing abstract design or hint at a field of wheat. (Photo: Daniel Rushall)

water-soluble pen or tailor's chalk to mark your line on the fabric. Gather a needle, small sharp scissors and cut a number of small cotton or wool tags as described in Chapter 1. You are ready to take your first steps.

When you start multiplying lines of ori-nui stitch and use it in groupings, you can see that this simple stitch produces magical results. Firstly, an array of four curved lines, starting close together at the top, and as they curve down the fabric the distance between them widens. This can suggest a track or other elements in a landscape or, augmented with other shibori stitches, gives a pleasing pattern for a scarf or runner. Then, simply using regimented rows of the stitch, spaced here at 2cm (¾in) apart, will create blocks of texture. Finally, ori-nui stitch can be formed into a much more organic arrangement. Use a variety of different lengths of the stitch, curved and straight, combined. A stunning plant-like design is created.

If you put together many random curved lines of varied lengths and spacing, you can bring to mind a delicate frond or tree design.

STEP-BY-STEP ORI-NUI STITCH

We will now take our very first stitches in shibori. This is the simplest method of working in shibori, but as I have already shown in groupings of this stitch, we open up many design and creative possibilities. Let us learn how to form this very basic building block of shibori.

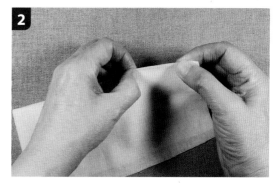

Take a plain piece of fabric and draw a straight line to guide where you will fold. You can use a ruler or draw freehand. Always draw lines to guide your stitching.

Fold the fabric along your marked line using your thumbnail and forefinger to make a sharp fold in the fabric. This will help you to follow the fold and not wander off your line as you stitch.

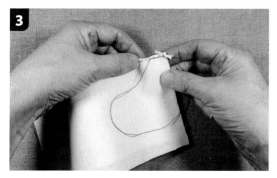

Prepare your double thread with a tag in the end. Then begin stitching 2mm (¹⁄₁₆in) away from the fold, through both layers of fabric. Maintain this regular distance away from the fold.

Finish stitching the whole row; stitch length can vary, but approximately 3mm (¹⁄₈in) long will give you a neat, regular pattern. You can experiment with varying the length of stitch and note what effect that has.

Begin gathering the fabric by pulling the stitches up using both strands of thread. Ease the fabric firmly but gently, back to the beginning of your row.

Ensure the stitches are arranged evenly, nestling evenly and tightly next to each other. Separate the two threads and tie another tag between the threads to secure the stitching.

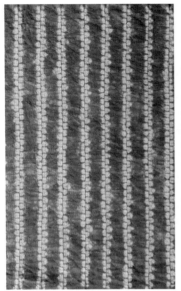

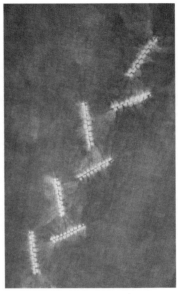

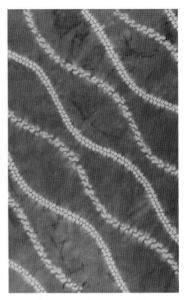

Ordered and regularly spaced lines of the stitch build a striking overall pattern. You can experiment with varying the spacing between the lines of stitching. This will give you a quite different feel.

Putting together short lengths of the stitch, just five or six stitches to a row, here arranged at an angle to each other, sets up another type of rhythm.

There are endless permutations of pattern when you curve lines of ori-nui and maki-nui stitch in a regular relationship to each other. Measure and draw your design on a grid before transferring to the fabric. The different effects of the two stitches set up a lovely rhythm.

Ideas for How the Stitch Can Be Put Together

Here are some further suggestions for ways to use this first building block of shibori. Firstly, we can create an overall striped piece of fabric. Here the multiple rows are about 2cm (¾in) apart. When these lines are then curved and make a modulated pattern in relationship to each other, there are many permutations of pleasing designs. Introducing an alternate line of maki-nui to each line of ori-nui creates yet another rhythm. With this kind of design, it is necessary to draw a grid and measure carefully. Another option is to take very short rows of stitch, just five or six stitches, and arrange them in different alignments to each other. This gives many creative possibilities. I have used this composition of rows to suggest grasses and other plant forms, but they can also be used to make striking abstract designs.

VARIATIONS ON ORI-NUI STITCH

Now we can start exploring the many innovative and ingenious possibilities of ori-nui stitch. We will look at taking the line of stitching away from the fold, and what pleasing arrangements can be made from just this simple alteration in stitching. We will also learn how to create maki-nui or oversew stitch, which again increases the design possibilities.

Then we can delve into what happens if we simply add an additional line of stitch around, parallel to, or adjacent to our first line. The permutations and design potential are endless.

Always remember to draw your design on to the fabric before starting to stitch. By making a line you can follow with your stitches, you are much more likely to achieve a satisfactory result.

Maki-Nui or Oversew Stitch

Maki-nui or oversew stitch makes a very attractive chevron-like, broken diagonal line. The thread rolls over the fold of fabric, the needle entering the fabric from the same side consistently. It is helpful to mark the fabric edge with small dots to ensure a regular design.

Some beautiful variations of design are made by using ori-nui and maki-nui in combination. The two types of stitches create an interesting rhythm. A most attractive line is made by sewing a line of maki-nui 3mm (¹/₈in) from the fabric edge and then immediately underneath sew a line of ori-nui 5mm (³/₁₆in) from the edge.

Fold the fabric along your line and mark the fabric fold with little dots 8–9mm (⁵/₁₆in) apart and 3mm (¹/₈in) from the fold edge.

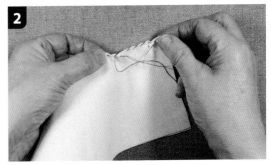

Begin stitching 3mm (¹/₈in) away from the fold, inserting the needle through the first dot, taking the needle and thread over the fold and inserting the needle into the next dot along.

Continue stitching in this way. You will find you can gather the fabric onto the needle 5 or 6 stitches at a time. Pull the thread through and go along to the next dot on the fold.

Stitch the whole row, always entering the fabric from the front. The marked dots will have ensured a regular pattern.

Gather up the row with the stitches arranged evenly, nestling tightly next to each other. Separate the two threads and tie another tag between the threads to secure the stitching.

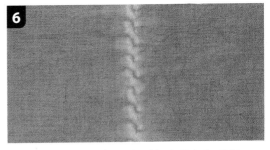

A completed and dyed row of maki-nui stitch. A satisfying and delicate diagonal line has been created. Experiment with different spacing of dots and distance away from the line to achieve other effects.

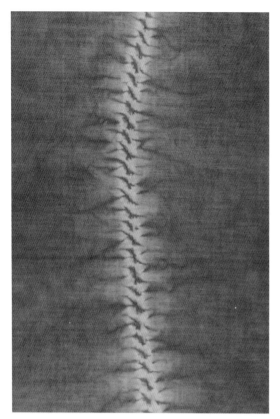

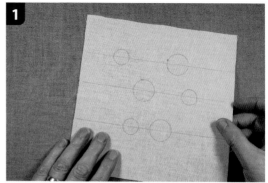

Draw three varyingly spaced lines onto the fabric and, using the end of your cotton reel or similar shape, intersperse circles along the lines. Vary the spacing between the circles to make a pleasing arrangement.

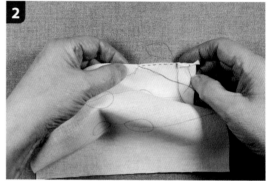

This attractive line, sewn on a folded cloth, uses an inner row of maki-nui 3mm (¹/₈in) from the fabric edge and then immediately underneath there is a line of ori-nui sewn 5mm (³/₁₆in) from the edge.

Crease the fold between thumb and forefinger, and begin the stitching 2mm (¹/₁₆in) away from the fold. Then at the first circle take your stitching away from the fold, following the line around the half circle.

Take the Stitched Line Away from the Fold

When starting a stitched line close to the fold and then taking it away from the fold, many further stimulating pattern possibilities are created. The curve away from the line pushes the fabric up and its surface area is easily dyed. In this example, we are going to insert small circles along the straight lines. You will need a piece of cotton fabric 20 × 20cm (8 × 8in), a ruler and cotton reels of different sizes to make the circles, plus your fabric marker.

We can apply this idea to form a pleasing and effortless pattern inspired by the natural world. Using this method of taking the line away from the fold, we can accomplish a

Sew all around the half circle and before you reach the fold, bring your stitching line back to 2mm (¹/₁₆in) away from the fold. Continue in this way for every circle until you finish the row.

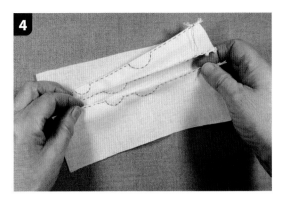

This process is repeated for all your lines and circles until the stitching is complete and you have three rows of stitching through three folds of fabric. Remember to be systematic and start each row from the same side of your square of fabric.

Carefully gather each row of stitching, pulling to the end, inserting a tag to secure it. You will see the circles pop up above the lines, which will enable the dye to reach the design.

After dyeing and unpicking the stitches, this is what you will achieve; a completed piece of fabric showing the singular effect of taking the stitched line away from the fold.

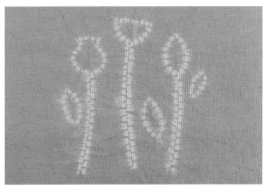

An arrangement of three flower shapes and leaves using the easy technique of taking the line of stitching away from the fold and then bringing it back to the fold.

simple arrangement of flowers. We begin to see how easily different designs and patterns are built up.

Adding One Additional Line of Stitching

Finally, let us explore what happens when you add one additional line of stitching. Another row of stitching is added close to, inside or next to another ori-nui or maki-nui line.

There are a few things to take note of before starting. The first is to take care to avoid catching the stitching of the first line with the needle when making the second line of stitches. Also, it is very helpful to use two colours of thread. And finally, the importance of creasing the fabric along the line you are going to sew is particularly important when stitching a curved line.

Adding this extra row opens up umpteen opportunities for further design ideas using this simple stitch. The pattern we will make together is a simple meadow of flowers and grasses; a frieze that could be repeated around the bottom of a blouse or T-shirt to great effect.

Use a piece of fabric 24 × 36cm (9 × 14in). As a guide to the scale of the design, the longest flower is 15cm (6in) tall.

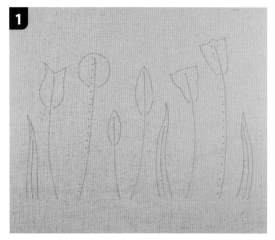

On a piece of fabric 24 x 36cm (9 x 14in) draw an arrangement of six flower shapes and three grasses with the water-soluble marker. As a guide to the scale of the design, the tallest flower is 15cm (6in).

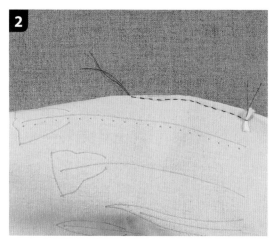

Working from the right-hand edge of the design, stitch the grass fronds. Create a sharp fold in the fabric, folding along the central line of the grass. The stitching is made 5mm (³/₁₆in) away from the fold. This line is gradually tapered off to take the last stitch through the edge of the fold.

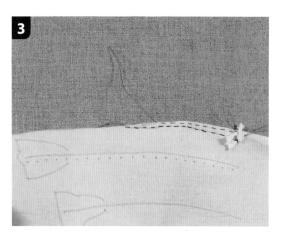

Using a different colour thread, stitch another row 2mm (¹/₁₆in) away from the fold above the first row of stitches. Taper off the row of stitching, taking the last stitch through the edge of the fold.

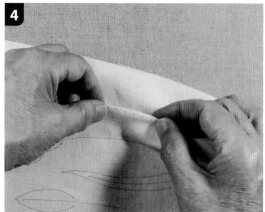

Next, we are stitching a flower. Using thumb and forefinger create a sharp fold in the fabric. When the line you are stitching is curved, it is very important to do this to ensure you follow the curve when stitching.

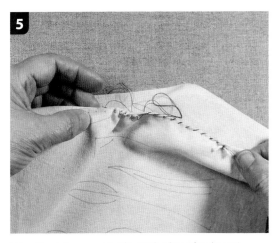

5

Using the dots as your guide, stitch a line of maki-nui/oversew stitch 3mm (¹/₈in) away from the fold. Always insert the needle from the front of the fabric, gathering the fabric onto the needle.

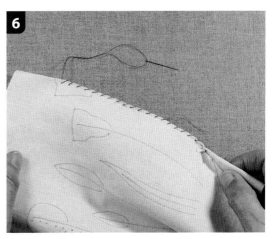

6

Continue the stitching 3mm (¹/₈in) away from the fold to just short of the top of the flower motif, leaving the tail of the thread for pulling up later.

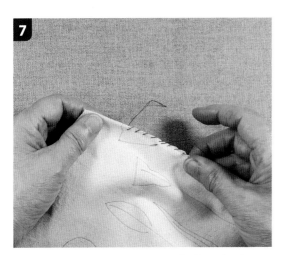

7

Use a different colour thread to create the flower head. Take the needle into the fabric just below the previous line of stitching, taking care not to catch the previous line of stitching with the needle.

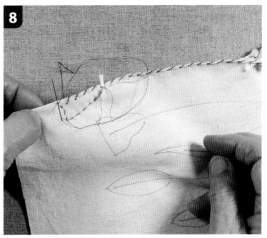

8

Continue to stitch along the outline of the flower head through both layers of fabric. Take the needle through the fold and leave for pulling up later.

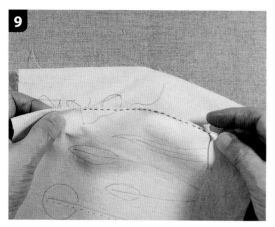

9

Now the next flower; stitch 2mm (¹⁄₁₆in) away from the fold in simple running stitches to just short of the top of the flower motif, leaving the tail of the thread for pulling up later.

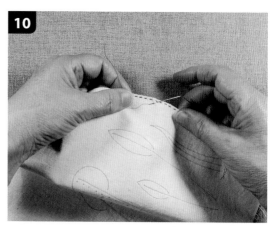

10

To create the flower head, take the needle into the fabric just below the previous line of stitching, taking care not to catch this stitch.

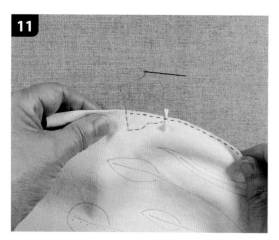

11

Continue to stitch along the outline of the flower head through both layers of fabric. Take the needle through the fold and leave for pulling up later.

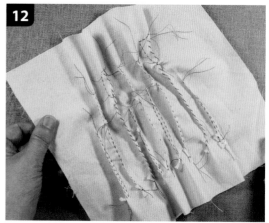

12

Here is the completed stitched fabric. Each flower and grass frond is made exactly the same as in steps 2 to 11. Note how all the stitching is made in the same direction from bottom to top of the fabric.

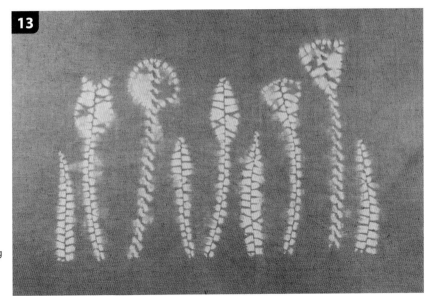

13

The finished pattern after dyeing with madder; a delightful but simple design that can be created by adding just an additional line of stitching close to, inside, or next to another ori-nui or maki-nui line.

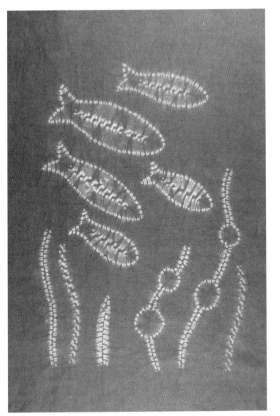

An engaging design of fish and seaweed; this design uses all the stitches and ideas we have explored and practised throughout the chapter. Fabric dimensions are 38 × 25cm (15 × 10in).

We can create leaves, flower heads, fish, fruit and grasses by adding an additional line. There are so many ideas and patterns to explore. Here is just one final project that we can make – an underwater scene. The design uses all the stitches we have explored in this chapter. The pattern is quite simple, but very effective. The golden rule with a slightly more complicated project is to always stitch all your lines in one direction. This ensures that you will not miss gathering up one row, which unfortunately can spoil the overall effect.

CHAPTER 4

AWASE ORI-NUI SHIBORI

Some shibori stitch techniques are not so much stars in their own right, but a great support act for all the other designs. Awase ori-nui is one of those stitches. In this chapter we will explore how to make this stitch and the ways in which we can use it to create and build up some inspirational patterns and images.

Awase ori-nui is another way of creating a line in shibori, and it is an interesting decorative stitch just on its own. This big and bold stitch is most useful to enhance and complement other shibori elements in a design.

This is one of the first stitches I used when discovering shibori and, used in combination with other stitches, it has great potential. It can be made slim and neat, or fat and chunky. The former is wonderful for stems or flower petals, and the latter is great to create a frame or border to another motif.

In this chapter I will show you how, by carefully tapering the line of stitching, you can create really effective but simple leaf and plant shapes. Also, using the stitch in multiple clusters and compositions promises further potential for creativity. Awase ori-nui can create interesting overall patterns and textures. It can be used to suggest a stem or a part of

The stitch is used here in a pleasing and striking manner to create a bold stem for a series of leaves. The fabric must be carefully manipulated when making a curved line in awase ori-nui.

◄ A landscape triptych with bold lines of awase ori-nui repeated across the cloth, suggesting field patterns. (Photo: Daniel Rushall)

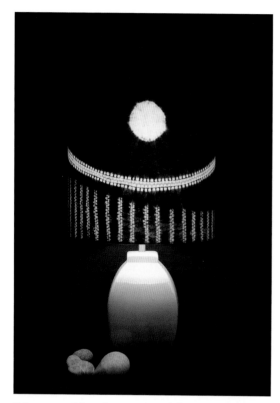

Using a curved line of awase ori-nui shibori, along with a couple of other shibori techniques, it can suggest a line of the horizon in a landscape.

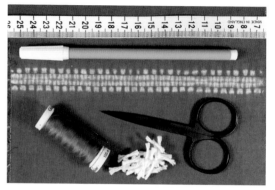

This is what you are aiming for, a finished and dyed line of awase ori-nui stitch shown alongside the basic tools required for making this stitch.

a landscape and is wonderful for building a decorative border. You will discover your own variations and arrangements over time.

This stitch is just a fraction more challenging to make than ori-nui, calling for a little more care in manipulating the fabric. First off, a pleat is made in the fabric and the needle is taken through all 4 layers of the fabric. Again, it needs little in the way of equipment, scissors, needles, and thread, but select two colours when making more complicated designs. A tape measure or ruler is most useful to help you make a regular and even pleat.

Firstly, let's look at how to make the stitch.

STEP-BY-STEP AWASE ORI-NUI STITCH

We will explore making this stitch in some simple step-by-step images. The fabric needs to be marked; a ruler is useful to measure three lines 5mm ($^3/_{16}$in) apart. Next fold into a pleat, scoring the fabric with thumb and finger to make the process of stitching easier. It will take a little practice to get an even line.

When gathering the fabric, ease the fabric back to the beginning of your row. Ensure the stitches are arranged evenly, to nestle evenly and tightly next to each other, before securing the stitching.

The stitch is particularly effective as a border, here shown around another simple design made with ori-nui shibori stitch.

Draw a line and then two more 5mm (³/₁₆in) away from the central line to create the dimensions of the pleat and to guide your stitching. Do experiment with increasing this measurement to see the effects achieved.

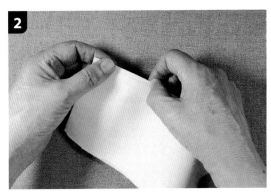

Fold the fabric right sides together along the central line you have drawn. On the reverse of the fabric, using thumbnail and forefinger, make a sharp fold in the fabric.

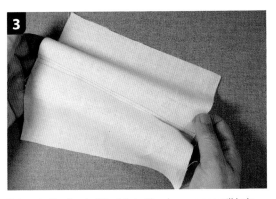

Return to the front of the fabric. The sharp crease will help you to follow the fold and not wander off your line as you stitch.

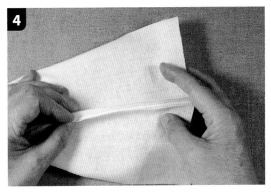

On the front of the fabric, following the two drawn lines either side of the central line, make creases in these using thumb and forefinger.

Prepare your double thread and commence stitching 2.5mm (¹/₈in) away from the fold, through four layers of fabric. Maintain this regular distance away from the fold.

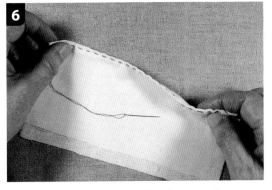

Stitch the whole row; your stitch length can vary, but approximately 3mm (¹/₈in) long will give you a neat regular pattern. Then gather the fabric, easing the fabric back to the beginning of your row. Ensure the stitches are arranged evenly, to nestle evenly and tightly next to each other. Secure the stitching.

VARIATIONS ON AWASE ORI-NUI

Once you have grasped the simple straight stitch, it is time to explore how the stitch can be varied by tapering the ends and grouping them together to make impressive and striking designs. In its simplest form, tapered at both ends awase ori-nui makes an excellent petal shape. Delightful flower and leaf shapes can easily be formed with this stitch.

Tapering the Pleat

Exactly the same principles apply as making a straight line of awase ori-nui. You draw a central line but the two lines either side are

A gold seven-petalled flower using awase ori-nui; the following instructions and images show how to make the flower.

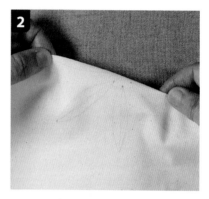

Working on the reverse of the fabric, using thumbnail and forefinger, make a sharp fold in the fabric along the centre line of each petal.

Returning to the front side of the fabric, working each petal one at a time, pinch together the very ends, pushing the centre fold down in between the two lips.

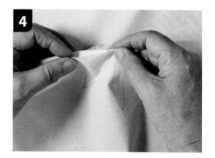

Continue along the length of the petal, creasing the fold between thumb and forefinger, and make a sharp fold.

Start each petal from the centre of the design. Begin the stitching on the very edge of the fold, just a fraction away from the beginning of the petal lip.

Gradually widen out the line of stitching to 3mm (¹/₈in) away from the fold, stitching through four layers of fabric. Continue in this way until the end of the petal.

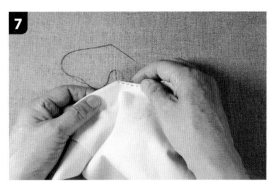

Follow the line of stitching to the very end, taking care to taper off the fold. Take the last stitch just beyond the point where the fold ends to bring the needle out through the fold of the fabric.

Repeat this for each of the other six petals. You will find it gets a little tricky and needs careful manipulation of the fabric as you add each petal. Always start the stitching at the centre of the design, with the thread ends at the outer edge.

Pull up each individual petal, carefully gathering the stitches and pulling to the end, then insert a tag to secure it.

tapered to finish on the fold. The stitching is started at the very edge of the fabric fold and gradually widens out as you reach the centre of the shape, and then tapers back again to finish at the other end. Always draw your shapes onto the fabric and follow the drawn lines carefully. This first pattern we will go through step by step is a seven-petalled flower. It is 15cm (6in) across. Draw the outline of the flower in water soluble marker pen. For each petal, draw a central line and make tapered shapes

either side, approximately 15mm (⁵/₈in) at the widest point.

Above and on the previous page we go through each stage of the process to make it completely clear.

There can be many distinct variations on this to create assorted designs. To create a broad leaf involves making a deeper fold in the fabric, which needs some careful manipulation. If you simply add a single bead (*see* Chapter 5) in the centre of the group of petals, a complete flower appears.

Another example of a flower created with this stitch; this time a simple bead is added to the centre and the flower has eight petals, like a celandine.

A horse chestnut leaf using awase ori-nui, along with a short length of ori-nui for the stem; here the curved shapes are larger, 3.5cm (1³/₈in) at the widest point. This is a little trickier to manipulate.

Creating an overall pattern

Awase ori-nui lends itself to be being put together in geometric arrangements, creating an overall pattern which can make stunning pillows, decoration for clothing or a quilt panel. There is a technique for sewing lots of short lengths of shibori together. This ensures that you are not having to stop and start stitch lengths, which would make the work become very confusing and fiddly.

This basketweave design is quite uncomplicated to produce. The images guide you through it step by step. Selecting two different colour threads for the two directions of stitch helps to prevent muddle and confusion. For the same reason, it is also important to start all stitching at one end of the fabric.

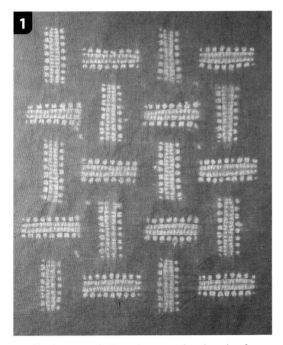

Dyed basketweave design using many short lengths of awase ori-nui at right angles to each other to create the pattern; this is worked on a piece of fabric 35 × 25cm (14 × 10in).

This is the grid for laying out the basketweave pattern. On paper, draw a grid of 2.5cm (1in) squares. On each block of four squares, draw a guide for sewing the awase ori-nui, each line 5 × 1cm (2 × 3/8in).

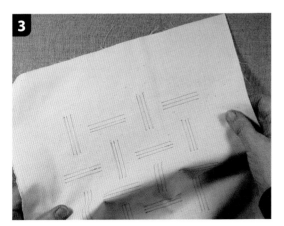

The alternating blocks of the pattern, transferred with a marker to the fabric. You should have three lines for each separate length of the stitch.

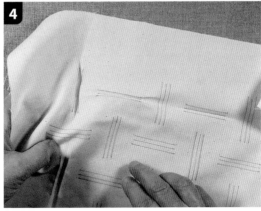

Begin creasing each drawn line, using thumb and forefinger, from the back of the fabric for the central line and from the front of the fabric for the outer two lines, to create a pleat.

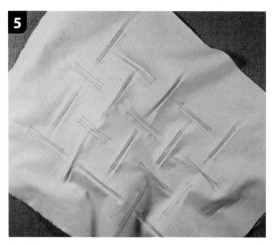

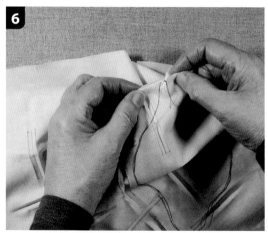

The fabric is prepared and ready for sewing. Each short length has been creased firmly to make an obvious and sharp pleat.

With double thread and a tag, begin the stitching in the top corner of the fabric, at the outer edge of the line. Cut a thread approximately 45cm (18in) long, enough to sew four of the blocks with one thread.

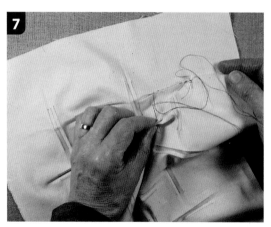

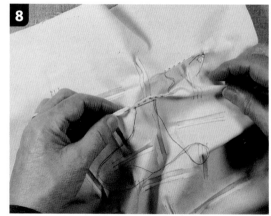

Sew 3mm (¹/₈in) away from the fold, through four layers of fabric. At the end of that block ensure the thread comes out at the bottom left corner, ready to enter the needle through the next horizontal block.

Follow this same pattern along the next block, bringing the needle out at the bottom left corner, ready to move onto the next horizontal block of stitches below.

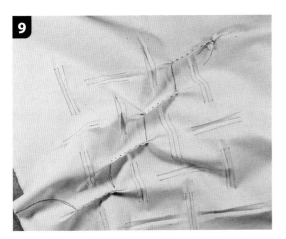

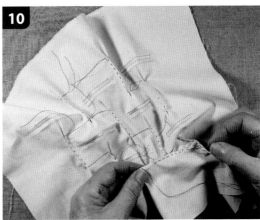

Here is one length of the horizontal blocks of awase ori-nui stitching completed. This shows how four short blocks can be sewn with one thread. Continue in this manner, grouping blocks of thread.

Once all the horizontal blocks have been stitched, continue with stitching all the vertical blocks of pleats. It will be helpful to use a different colour thread here. Again, link blocks of stitches together for ease of sewing.

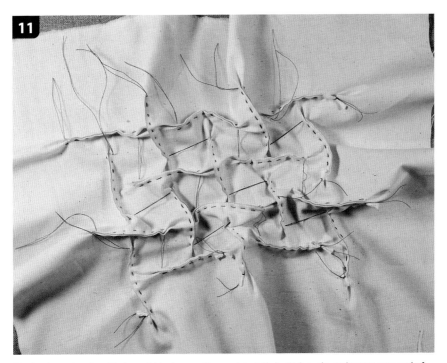

The horizontal and vertical small blocks are all completed. If all stitch ends are kept to one end of the fabric, it ensures a methodical way of working and is easier for the final gathering up of each block of stitches.

Simple Combination with Another Stitch Technique

As soon as you begin to think about adding another stitch technique alongside the awase ori-nui stitch, many individual and innovative arrangements can be formed. As you learn different stitches throughout the book, you will come up with some ingenious combinations.

Here is a step-by-step guide to creating the five-petalled flower with awase ori-nui and maki-nui. This flower design is formed in an 18cm (7¼in) diameter circle.

An example of using awase ori-nui in combination with a curved ori-nui line. An effective seaweed pattern is suggested with this collection of lines.

Another example of mixing awase ori-nui with another straightforward technique, maki-nui. A madder dyed five petalled flower. It is just one example of many combinations of stitch that can be put together. The design is created in an 18cm (7 ¼in) diameter circle.

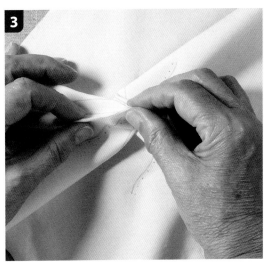

Add some dots for the maki-nui stitch at 8mm (⁵⁄₁₆in) apart. Each central line of the six petal shapes must be creased between thumb and forefinger on the back of the fabric.

On the front side of the fabric, working one petal at a time, pinch together the very ends, pushing the centre fold down in between the two lips.

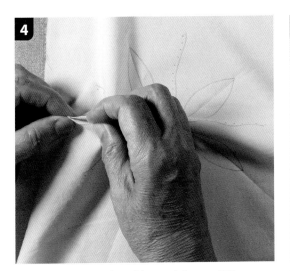

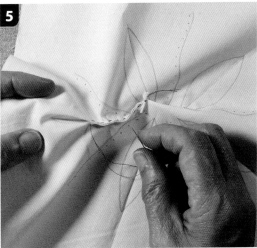

Continue to pinch the lips of the petal shape until the other end, ensuring that you make a good crease along the drawn lines.

Beginning from the middle of the design, start stitching on the very edge of the fold, and widen out the line of stitching to 3mm (⅛in) away from the fold, stitching through four layers of fabric.

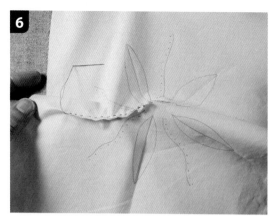

Continue the line of stitching to the very end, tapering off as you reach the end. The last stitch is made by bringing the needle out through the fold of the fabric.

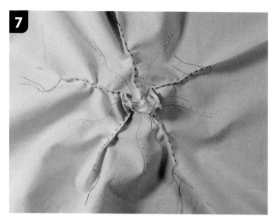

All six petals are stitched. Note how all rows of stitching start from the middle of the design. Always be methodical in the order of stitching.

The next step is to stitch the alternate maki-nui lines. Fold the fabric along your line and be sure to mark the fabric fold with little dots 8mm (5/16in) apart.

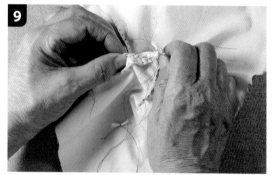

Begin stitching 3mm (1/8in) away from the fold, inserting the needle through the first dot, taking the needle and thread over the fold and inserting the needle into the next dot along. You can gather the fabric onto the needle, five or six stitches at a time.

Each row of stitching is complete, the oversewn maki-nui stitch and the awase ori-nui stitch. All threads for pulling up are on the outside of the design for ease of gathering. The design will need gathering and securing of each thread before dyeing.

CHAPTER 5

NE-MAKI, BOSHI AND GUNTAI SHIBORI

This is an exciting and useful set of techniques to build your shibori skills. This group of techniques are all a kind of binding. In these ways of working, the process involves tying or stitching very tightly. They are most useful for adding special details to a design such as seeds, a presence in the sky, small leaves or lines. They are less useful for creating a complete design in their own right.

Ne-maki is the art of making small circles by tying a small bead or other object into the cloth, leaving a dark dyed centre with a white circle around. Boshi shibori is a further development of this, stitching a small circle and using a 'core' to gather the shape around and capping or covering with a small piece of plastic, which keeps the dye out completely. With this method you can make totally white shapes in your cloth. Guntai is an oversew stitch which is used to gather the fabric as you proceed, particularly useful for small, elongated shapes such as ribbons, petals or leaves.

We will look at each of these processes in turn and the straightforward materials needed for each.

NE-MAKI SHIBORI

This is the action of tying different-sized objects into the cloth and then binding with a strong cotton string. Put simply, how many times one

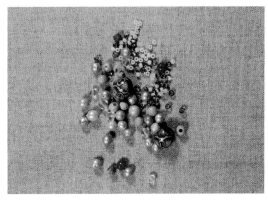

A selection of beads collected for tying into the fabric. Sizes to collect vary between 3mm ($^1/_8$in) to 1cm ($^3/_8$in).

◀ This design of holly leaves with berries shows how ne-maki and guntai shibori can work together to create designs from the natural world.

binds the thread around and what size bead is selected will produce a different-sized resist circle.

You need to make a collection of beads, varying in size. In the blue dyed sample, the bead sizes used vary between 3mm ($^1/_8$in) to 1cm ($^3/_8$in), but the majority of the beads are my favourite size for using to sprinkle around my designs, around 4mm ($^3/_{16}$in) in diameter.

The designs made inside the bound circles are completely random. They can look like a flower, a bird or sometimes a butterfly! I love the possibilities of these small star-like dots to decorate the surface, as well as their usefulness as seeds or plant pods. There is much pleasure in the effect achieved by using this easy technique.

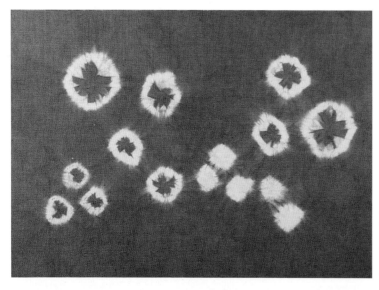

A selection of different-sized beads and the effect they have. Note the randomly created centre pattern. The completely white shapes are made by binding a small piece of plastic over the bead.

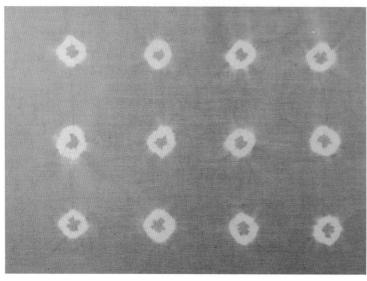

Tying the beads in straight lines, evenly spaced apart gives a very pleasing rhythm and provides a foundation for an abstract shibori design.

Step-by-Step Ne-Maki

Here we will look at this straightforward method of tying a bead in. It is important to note that the bead is always placed on the reverse of the fabric, and it is good practice to stitch the beads in place before starting any other shibori stitching.

Overleaf are examples of how I use ne-maki to enhance flower and seedhead designs, combined with other stitches. In all these examples, the beads were attached to the reverse of the fabric, then the other parts of the design were stitched using ori-nui, guntai and miru shibori. The final binding of the beads is left until this stitching is complete. But at the gathering stage the beads are bound first, then the other stitching is pulled up afterwards.

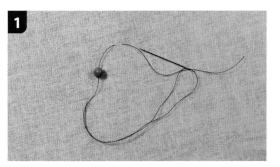

Take a small stitch in the reverse of the fabric and thread the selected bead onto the needle.

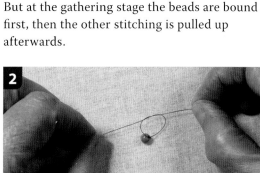

Make a simple reef knot. The bead needs to be held firmly in place while you are doing other stitching.

The bead is safely attached to the reverse of the fabric. This is the time to make all your other shibori stitching before binding.

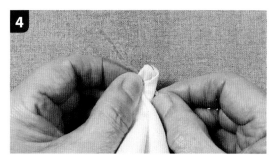

On the front of the fabric, gather the fabric tightly and evenly around the bead. Place the binding thread behind, leaving a tail to tie up later.

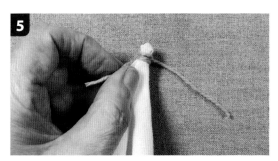

Wrap the thread around the bead three or four times; the number of times the thread is wrapped around produces a smaller or larger circle.

Finish off by tying a reef knot to secure the wrapping tightly in place.

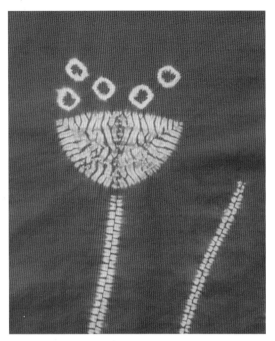

Here an example of ne-maki is used to enhance a flower head; a scattering of five beads decorates the flower.

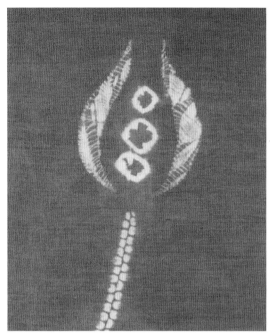

Here the beads are enclosed within the design, suggesting a section through a seed pod.

A mass of small ne-maki shapes to hint at the seeds of a hogweed flower.

BOSHI

This is a method of making large circles and shapes but keeping the dye out of the shape completely. Creating with boshi shibori involves finding larger round items to wrap the fabric around, such as lengths of balsa wood or old cotton reels. Alternatively, you can make your very own 'core' out of fabric scraps. They are fun to make and as they have some give in them, they are more secure when the binding thread is wrapped around the fabric.

The boshi process is a little involved. The shape required is stitched around, then select or make a core of the correct size and shape to gather around. The fabric is gathered and tied around the core, and finally covered with a small piece of plastic and tightly bound with cord.

I mainly use boshi shibori to create a sun or moon shapes on my fabric, but it is possible to make odd shapes too. The shapes need to be reasonably simple.

A very large boshi circle, 24cm (9½in) in diameter. Note how some colour has seeped in around the edges, which can happen. It was decorated after dyeing with vintage buttons to suggest dandelion seeds.

This textile shows examples of creating odd boshi shapes, a part circle which is made in the same way as a whole circle. These shapes need more careful manipulation.

Making a Core for Boshi Shibori

Let's discover how to create these small cores. I find them a fun thing to make. They are a great way to use up small lengths of scrap fabric. You need a piece of light cotton fabric. The size of the fabric scrap depends on what size the final core needs to be. I suggest creating a few different sizes. They can be used again and again, though it is a good idea to only use them with one colour dye pot, as the dye could transfer.

We will make a 2cm (¾in) core from a 27cm (11in) piece of fabric in this demonstration. This will comfortably make a circle 6cm (2¼in) in diameter.

A selection of cores of different sizes used to make the boshi designs. I love the way they absorb the dye in parts, becoming interesting objects in themselves. There is also an example of a length of balsa wood.

To make a 2.5 × 2cm (1 × ¾in) core take a piece of fabric 27 × 10cm (11 × 4in). Mark four equally spaced parallel lines.

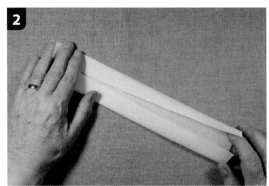

Fold along the lines and bring the outside edges to the centre line. Crease and fold sharply using your thumbnail and forefinger.

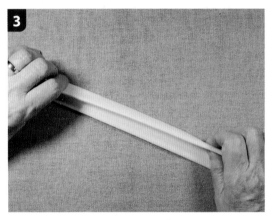

Fold these two folds again along the centre line, onto each other, creating a piece of fabric four folds thick.

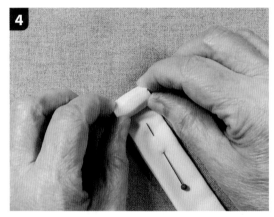

Use a pin to hold the four layers of fabric together as you begin to tightly roll these layers into a core.

Once all the fabric is rolled up, trim the four fabric layers level before beginning to sew. Hold the roll firmly, making a first stitch to secure the end of the roll.

Continue stitching and securing the fabric ends using a long stitch until the whole of the loose end is firmly secured. You have made a fabric core to make a circle 6cm (2¼in) in diameter.

How to Create a Shape in Boshi Shibori

We will look at the technique to make a completely white resist in the fabric. You will need a fabric core you have made, or find something of 2cm (¾in) in diameter to gather the fabric around, plus a small sample of fabric 20cm (8in) square.

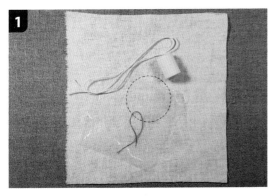

Draw a circle about 6cm (2¼in) and stitch around the circle. Cut a piece of plastic 10 × 10cm (4 × 4in), choose your core and a length of strong cord long enough to go around four or five times.

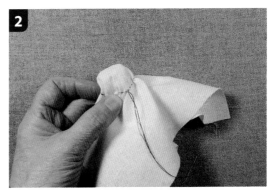

Place the core on the underside of the fabric, in the centre of the stitched circle and gather the thread tightly, ensuring the fabric is pleated evenly.

Wind the surplus stitch thread around the stitching and tie off with a reef knot as securely as possible.

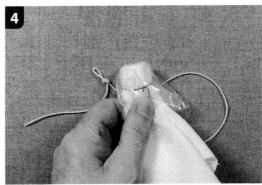

Place the plastic capping over the gathered shape. Make a loop in the binding cord and place it around the shape.

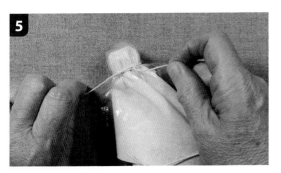

Thread the other end of the cord through the loop, and make sure the binding is very tight and 'bites' the core.

Wrap the binding cord around five or six times and tie the ends together with a knot.

Accidents that Happen!

Sometimes the dye will seep into the fabric and leave a pale residue. This happens mainly with plant dyes, where the water is heated to a high temperature and the fabric is in the dye bath for a long time. It will also happen with fibre-reactive dyes. I rather love this effect!

This effect rarely happens with natural indigo.

It can be prevented by ensuring your fabric core is very tightly wrapped, or by additionally wrapping the core in plastic film.

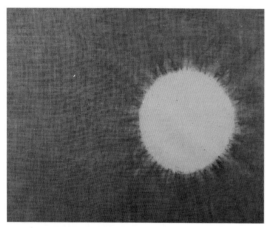

This is an example of an indigo blue dyed 10cm (4in) circle. This used a core of 5cm high × 3.5cm (2 x 1½in).

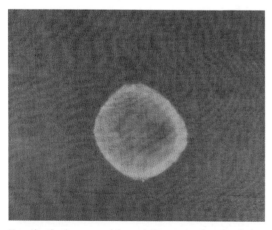

Here the dye has seeped through the core and made a halo effect of a paler version of the colour in the centre. This piece was dyed with onion skins, which required it to remain in the dyebath for a long time.

GUNTAI SHIBORI

Of the three ways of working in this chapter, guntai shibori can be used to create some attractive small designs, beautiful and complete in their own right. It can be used to compose some simple flower shapes, leaves, buds and particularly birds. Here are examples of some of these ideas.

The best designs and patterns to use guntai for are narrow shapes. It is possible to stitch fatter shapes, but I would then divide the shape into two, as I have done when stitching the holly leaves shown at the front of this chapter.

Random and narrow leaf shapes on a stem of ori-nui are the perfect kind of design to create with guntai shibori.

This delicate six-petalled flower shows how very natural, flowing shapes can be created with this stitch.

Another suitable subject for guntai, birds in flight. The body and the wings of the bird are stitched separately.

The stitch is a kind of oversew stitch because, as the stitching progresses, the fabric rolls in on itself. The advantage of this stitch is that it is complete in itself, and there is no need to come back and pull it up. But the biggest disadvantage of the technique is the care needed when unpicking. This is best done with a seam ripper, working on the reverse side of the fabric. It greatly helps to use a contrasting colour thread from the final dye colour.

Tips for Dyeing Guntai

Something to take note about guntai shibori is that it is most successful with natural indigo and good results can also be achieved using Rit dyes. Unfortunately, with fibre-reactive and natural plant dyes there is a tendency for too much colour to seep into the stitching and the results are rather disappointing. Not enough distinct white is left.

How to Create Guntai Stitch Step by Step

Let us explore step by step how to make the stitch. A sharp clear drawing is imperative. This enables you to see the shape clearly and follow the line easily. Use a double thread that is three times the length of the finished shape, although it is possible to join another thread in as the stitching progresses. The stitch is spaced approximately 2mm ($^1/_{16}$in) apart. As shown, start and finish with a tag, as it helps at the unpicking stage.

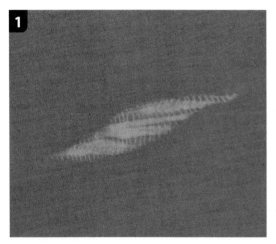

A simple leaf or petal shape which we will create in stages, step by step.

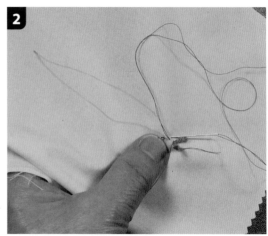

A clear outline is important. A tag is again used to anchor the thread. Use a thread three times the length of the shape, though you can join a thread partway through. The stitching starts at the end point of the shape.

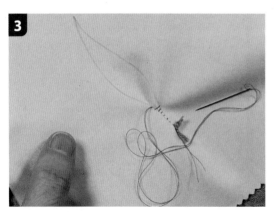

Working from left to right, take the needle in at an angle. Continue in this way, pulling the stitching tightly every four or five stitches. The distance between the stitches is approximately 2mm ($^1/_{16}$in) measured along the edge.

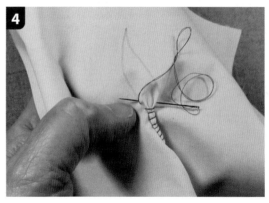

It gets more difficult to follow the drawing/line as the stitching of the shape progresses, because the fabric gathers and bunches as you stitch.

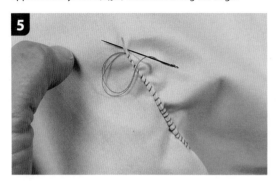

The stitches can be wider apart at the widest point of the shape. But as you get to the other end, make the stitches smaller again.

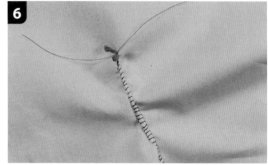

Tie off with a tag; it is possible to do a small stitch to finish, but the tag is very helpful when unpicking. The biggest challenge with guntai stitch is the unpicking after dyeing.

Lettering

Another most effective way of using guntai shibori is to create lettering. It is best to find a typeface that is rounded in style as the example shown here. An angular typeface would be difficult to stitch. It will be necessary to adapt the lettering, perhaps making it wider in places and eliminating too many flourishes.

Guntai shibori can be used most successfully to produce lettering. Find a typeface that is quite organic in shape and design.

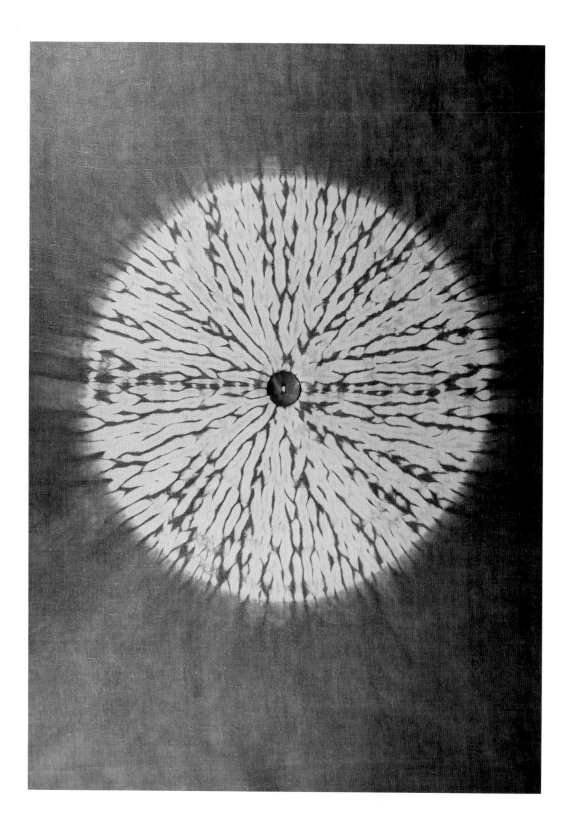

CHAPTER 6

MIRU SHIBORI

This technique, miru shibori, is my overall favourite. Whenever I use it in my designs, this way of working gives me such great pleasure. This is in some way because the final pattern (the textural markings, not the shape) achieved is always random. The shape itself is clearly determined by your outline. The irregularly spaced stitches in each row build up to a flowing arbitrary pattern, radiating out from the centre of the design.

Miru shibori is used when an overall regular shape is wanted; that is, a motif that is the same on both sides, like a circle or a square, diamond or oval. The stitching is worked through two layers of folded fabric. The texture, constructed from multiple rows of stitching, builds interest and pattern just by itself.

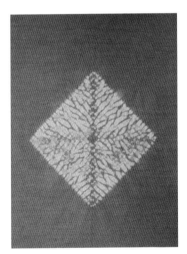

A miru diamond pattern, 12cm (4³/₄in) along each side, dyed with chemical dyes. Draw the shape accurately first and then fold in two to provide an even-looking design. This design is stitched with two needles from the diamond's point.

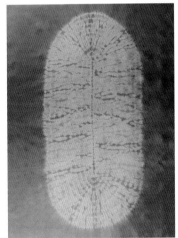

An oval on silk in miru shibori, 45cm (18in) long. Silk is a slippery customer to work with. It is helpful to tack the two halves of fabric together to prevent the design going out of shape. This oval is natural plant dyed with madder root.

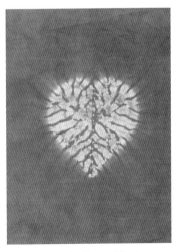

A good example of a suitable shape for miru shibori is a small heart shape. It is just 7cm (2³/₄in) across. As long as both sides of your design are the same – that is, a regular motif – miru shibori is the perfect technique to use.

◀ A large miru circle dyed with indigo on a chunky linen cloth. This shows the beautiful patterning that is a hallmark of this technique.

Additionally, miru shibori is most suitable to create designs in nature, flower heads, leaves, fruits and seedheads. These wonderful textures can suggest the cup of an acorn, veins of leaves, or florets of a daisy. You will be able to discover many more natural designs that will be suitable as an inspiration for using this stitch. It can be successfully used to create the texture of a sea creature – a turtle or a crab, for instance. But here it would need to be combined with other stitches. We will look at some ideas for this in a future chapter.

Furthermore, the stitched shapes can be combined together to make a complete flower with many petals or a segmented seedhead.

STEP-BY-STEP MIRU SHIBORI STITCH

Miru shibori is worked on folded fabric, sewing the design through two layers of fabric. The equipment needed is straightforward: thread, needles and pins, tags and a marker pen to draw the design. When making the original drawing, you will get much better results if you draw the whole shape onto your piece of fabric, and then fold it in half. It is necessary to pin the two folds of fabric. This is so they do not slip when stitching and distort the shape and is particularly important for geometric shapes such as circles, ovals and diamonds. If using

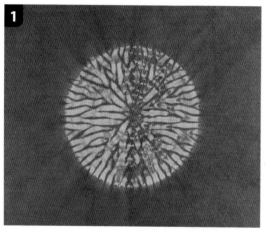

A 12cm (4³/₄in) miru circle with a step-by-step explanation. The circle needs to be drawn as a whole on the cloth, then fold the fabric in half matching outline to outline. This makes certain that it is a true circle, not a slightly wonky one.

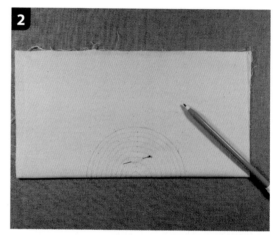

The half circle is marked with all the lines to be sewn marked at 6–7mm (¹/₄in) apart. As long as the outside line and the centre circle are accurately placed, the other lines can waver a little. The cloth needs to be pinned to hold the two halves of fabric firmly while you sew.

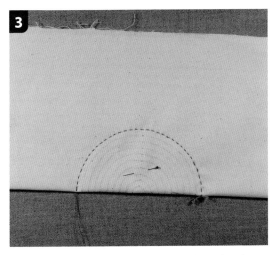

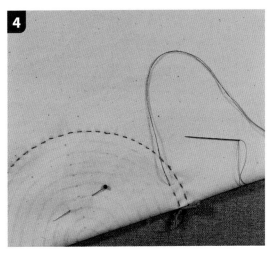

Start stitching on the outside row of the circle and work inwards. Make sure this outer row of stitches is neat and small and follows your outline accurately. Inner rows can be a little more slipshod, but ensure the smallest inner circle is in the middle.

Along the folded edge, stagger the first stitch at the beginning of each consecutive row, to ensure a random design. Additionally, vary the length of stitch between 3–6mm ($\frac{1}{8}$ –$\frac{1}{4}$in) long.

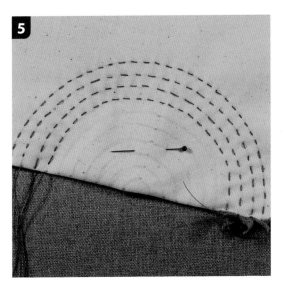

Four rows of stitching are now finished, showing how the stitches at the beginning and ending of each row are staggered at the fold edge. Also note how all stiches are staggered in relation to the previous row.

The stitching is complete for the whole circle. Note a neat outer row and the rather more haphazard inner rows, but the small inner circle is accurately placed in the centre of the circle. Long threads are left for pulling up.

silk, it is necessary to baste the two halves of the fold together to prevent the shape distorting.

Sometimes the line of the fold can appear very discernible. This feature can be utilised; for example, when making a leaf, a central vein can be created. The visibility of the fold can be minimised by staggering the start of stitches every alternate row. Moreover, the other way of reducing this noticeable effect is by making sure the stitching is gathered really tightly.

Sewing the Miru Stitch

Learn to make a miru shibori circle as shown on the previous page. The average distance between rows on miru shibori is 6–7mm ($^1/_4$in). Please note that the distance between the rows of stitches will be closer on silk or very fine cotton, about 5mm ($^3/_{16}$in), and further apart, about 9mm ($^3/_8$in), on a heavy linen. The distance between the rows of stitching can be played with to achieve other patterns.

Gathering the Miru Shape

The gathering of miru shapes is very important as they must be pulled up evenly to get the complete stunning effect. All the threads need to be pulled together to ensure the fabric is fully gathered back to the starting point. Check and check again when gathering that it is pulled up as tightly as absolutely possible. Then, starting at the shortest length at the top, each thread is tied off individually with a tag.

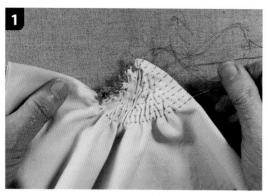

Begin gathering the threads, holding all the thread ends and pulling them up together. Ease the fabric firmly but gently, back to the beginning of each row.

By pulling the stitches up all together it ensures that each and every row is gathered fully back to the start. If all the stitches are not fully gathered, it spoils the overall pattern.

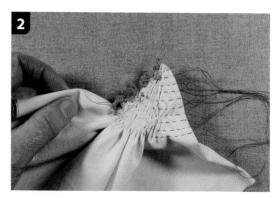

Trim the threads back to 8cm (3in) for ease of handling. Row by row, give a final pull, separate the two threads and tie a tag into the end of each row of stitches.

Work methodically down the cloth to be certain that you do not miss a row, until all the threads are gathered and firmly secured, ready for dyeing.

MORE MIRU IDEAS

A leaf is a simply stunning pattern to make with miru. There are so many different leaf shapes in nature to inspire us: beech leaves, hazel leaves and ivy leaves to name a few shapes that can be successfully translated into shibori.

There is a lot of stitching involved when filling a whole shape with stitches. However, it is possible to stitch just three or four rows around a shape, as in the example of the poppy seedhead. This is also most pleasing. You could play around with some shapes full of stitching and some only outlined with a few rows.

If the stitches are started a little way away from the fold, many other permutations can be achieved. It is particularly successful when used in a leaf shape to suggest the central vein or two halves of a seed pod.

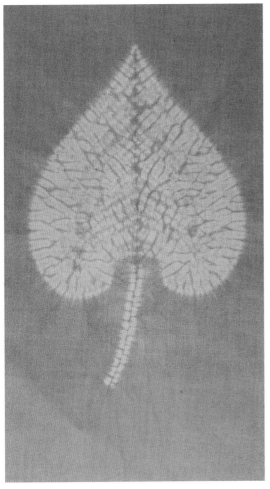

A leaf is the perfect type of design to make in miru shibori. As a guide, this leaf is 11.5cm (4¹/₂in) long without the stem. The great variety of leaf shapes found in nature can be successfully created with miru. Adding an ori-nui line defines the stem. Stitched on fine cotton lawn, the rows are 5mm (³/₁₆in) apart.

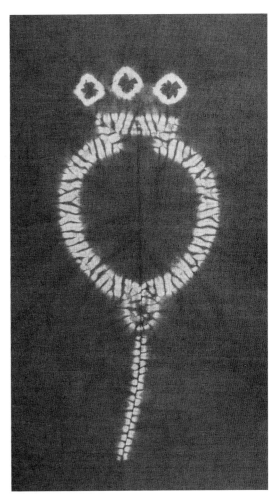

Here is an alternative way of using miru shibori, by constructing an outline with three or four lines of stitching and leaving the centre empty. This poppy seedhead is formed on the fold with only a few rows to define its shape. This way of creating has many design possibilities.

Another possibility is to start the stitching just a little distance away from the fold, leaving a line between the two halves. Here is a collection of wool cushions of different leaf shapes with a central vein created by leaving a space along the fold.

How To Make a Leaf Step by Step

Let us look at how to make this lime leaf with a central stem and stalk, step by step. The best result will be achieved if the leaf is drawn as a whole, sketched on some paper. Then fold the paper and trace a half onto the fabric. Mark a line 4mm (³/₁₆in) from the fabric fold to create the central vein, and start the stitching along this line. It is important to follow the outer line very carefully with the stitching. The inner stitching rows are not so crucial.

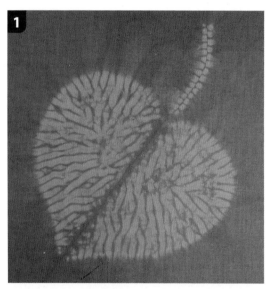

A classic lime leaf shape in miru shibori where the stitching of the folded fabric is started 4mm (³/₁₆in) away from the fold, creating the effect of a central vein. As in all miru patterns, it is preferable to draw your leaf whole to guarantee a pleasing design.

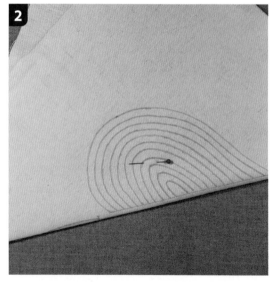

Draw the pattern on paper and mark the lines of the rows. Then transfer the design onto the fabric along with all the row markings. As a guide, the design shown here is 15cm (6in) high and 18cm (7in) at the widest point.

3

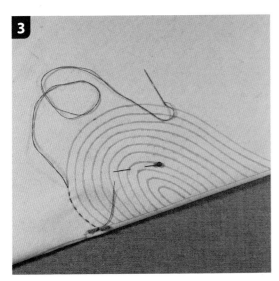

Use a pin to hold the two halves of fabric together. The stitches begin on the outside of the leaf and a measured distance away from the fold. Ensure this outer row is neat, following the outline accurately.

4

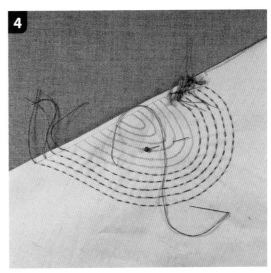

Continue in this way, stitching all the inner rows. Remember to stagger the stitches as much as possible in each row in relation to the previous row, to achieve the desired random patterning.

5

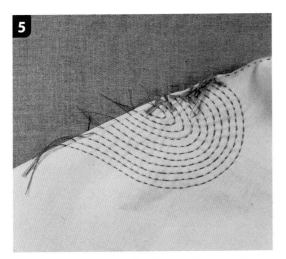

Once all the body of the leaf has been stitched, a small stem in ori-nui stitch is added from the base of the leaf. Begin the stitching at the base of the leaf and stitch away from the leaf.

6

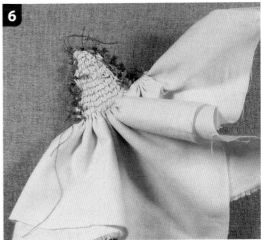

All stitching must be carefully gathered, easing the fabric firmly but gently back to the absolute beginning of each row. Then tie the rows to secure them ready for dyeing.

MULTIPLES OF MIRU MOTIFS

Miru shibori patterns get even better when they are grouped together. This can involve repeating exactly the same size motif a few times within a circle or square. Alternatively, you can place different proportioned shapes along a line or scatter them across the cloth.

Designs Using Multiples of Repeat Shapes

Many more design possibilities open up as soon as we begin to put a number of regular and repeated miru shibori shapes together. They can be combined in threes, fours or fives. More than that number and the cloth does become rather

A shamrock leaf is made using three repeated miru shapes. Each of the segments are pinned and sewn separately. To create the effect of the vein, the stitching is started a short distance away from the fold.

fiddly to sew and manipulate. And also, more challenging to ensure the stitched shapes are fully gathered.

Using a number of the same shapes together makes a whole series of other designs achievable. There are a couple of examples shown here, a shamrock and a five-sided star. It is another method of making many petalled flowers. That is a design we will look at in detail.

Making A Multi-Part Shape Step by Step

Here are step-by-step instructions for a four-petalled flower with a bead at the centre. After transferring the drawing to the fabric, each petal is stitched in turn. Remember to always work the stitching from the centre of the flower outwards.

A five-sided star is a good example of using repeat modules of the same shape in miru shibori. The star is constructed in an 18cm (7in) circle. Each spine of the star is made of three rows of stitching.

A four-petalled flower, using repeated miru shapes and a small bead to create the flower centre. Step-by-step instructions follow.

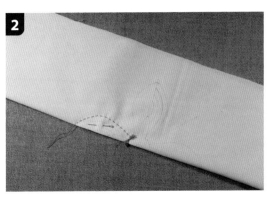

Start with one petal and pin to hold the folded fabric. Stitch the outer row of stitching first. Always start the stitching from the centre of the design and work outwards.

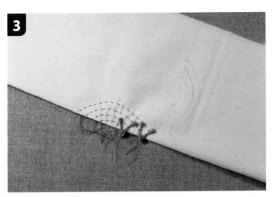

Each petal is made from four rows of stitching. Note that a small space is left in the centre of each petal, the stitching starting away from the fold.

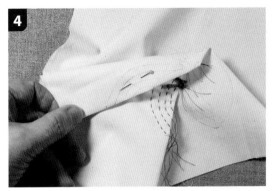

Then proceed to the next petal and follow the same procedure, folding along the centre line and pinning to hold in place, before sewing.

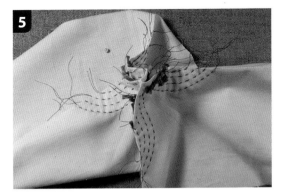

Work around the design, stitching each petal in turn. Select a small bead to insert in the centre on the reverse of the fabric.

Bind the small bead, then proceed to gather each row of stitching and tie each row off. With multiple shapes, the gathering is intricate. This is why it is important to stitch from the centre outwards.

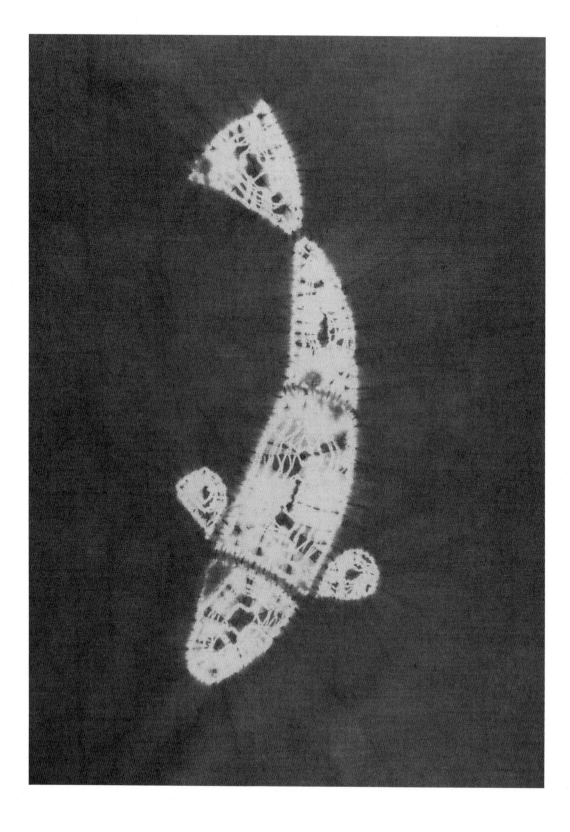

CHAPTER 7

MAKI-AGE SHIBORI

The next technique we are going to explore has many uses and applications. This method of working is most useful for building shapes that are irregular in outline. The odd shapes can be created with one outline of stitching. Additionally, these non-uniform shapes can be formed by putting together a number of segments.

In comparison to other techniques such as miru, it manages to exclude a large amount of dye. The shapes created are much whiter with some decorative texture. The crisscross thread creates a random arrangement of pattern radiating out from the shape's stitched outline. This effect is not controllable; the combination of binding, dye and chance create your finished pattern. When using maki-age you need to trust to chance a little more and be accepting of what happens.

The serendipitous nature of binding and dye penetration can often enhance the design by suggesting petal divisions or pattern. The textures created can bring to mind fish scales, seedhead husks or wing markings. This gives much potential for motif development.

Inspired by a magnolia flower, this clearly shows the use of irregular segmented shapes typical of maki-age shibori designs. Each petal outline is drawn accurately and then stitched around. With intricate and small shapes like these, a thinner, lighter weight fabric is preferable.

◀ An example of creating with maki-age, showing the interesting textures that can be achieved. This fish is 24cm (9¹⁄₂in) from nose to tail.

A design inspired by a woven tapestry fabric. The five odd-shaped petals with variegated but rounded edges are a perfect motif to create with this technique. Each of the five petals are stitched and bound separately.

A small butterfly, just 16cm (6¹/₂in) from the furthest tip of the wings, is the perfect pattern to try maki-age shibori. The wings are rounded and therefore quite easy to bind. It is combined with ori-nui stitch, as shown in Chapter 3, to create antennae and the body.

In maki-age shibori there are more elements of chance that can come into play.

When the design outline is very asymmetrical, particularly if it is long and thin, it is a challenge to gather and bind the whole shape fully. A small amount of dye can creep in at the pointed edge. I just accept this as part of the process and do not get bothered by it. The chance of this happening can be ameliorated by selecting simpler and rounder shapes.

When a shape is particularly complicated or irregular, it may be necessary to tie an additional binding thread around the base. After the binding is done, look to see if you can see some of the original stitches. If you can, add a short length of binding thread and cover those stitches.

A Few Words of Advice on Materials

When first attempting maki-age shibori it is preferable to use a fine cotton, that with a weight of 90g per square metre (2.6oz per sq yd). Using this weight fabric will give better results for the beginner. You will find it so much easier to manipulate and bind. For instance, I used a lighter weight fabric for the fish and the magnolia, as they have many divisions that are close together. The thicker the fabric used, the more challenging it is to bind completely.

For the binding, try both double weight thread and a fingering weight yarn. If you have sewn a small shape, use a thinner thread to bind it. In the next section we will look at the effects of different yarns.

MAKI-AGE BINDING TECHNIQUES

Three Different Binding Methods

Firstly, we are going to explore the different possibilities of binding and the effects made by each approach.

There are nuances within the way the cloth is bound that can vary the pattern produced. The fabric can be bound completely, covering the majority of the cloth, and excluding nearly all the dye. Or the binding can crisscross the gathered shape, allowing more of the dye to penetrate. This can be further varied by using

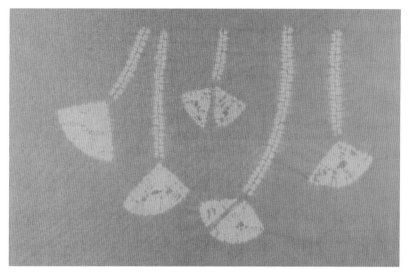

These dangling seedheads show how different ways of binding the cloth can subtly vary the pattern produced. The fabric can be bound completely, covering the majority of the cloth, and excluding nearly all the dye. Or the binding can crisscross the gathered shape, allowing more of the dye to penetrate.

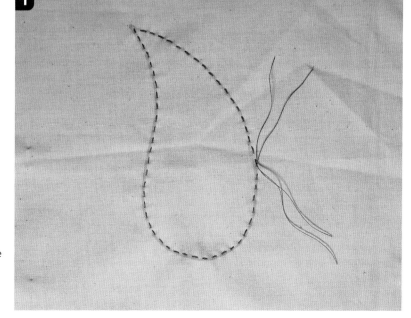

A strong clear outline is marked, and the paisley stitched around. This exact shape is repeated in the following images. Each shows the variation achieved with the use of diverse threads and a particular manner of binding. In all cases it measures 10cm (4in) tall.

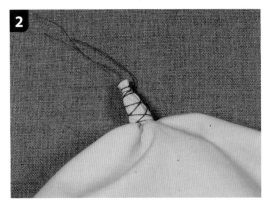

The first example here is bound with ordinary polyester sewing thread. This can be the thread you used to stitch around the shape. In this case, allow an extra length of thread when preparing the stitching thread.

The design produced with fine ordinary sewing thread allows for the maximum amount of dye to penetrate the bound shape. The original outline stitching is obvious. Also note the thin spidery pattern of lines and compare this with the following sample.

In the second example, our paisley outline is bound with a chunkier cord, string, or double-knit weight yarn. This has the effect of excluding more dye from the cloth as the yarn used is thicker.

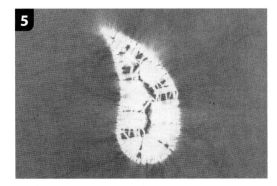

The design produced with a thick thread resists a larger amount of dye. The pattern produced is whiter and the original outline stitching is less obvious. Note the more substantial marks left by this type of thread.

In the third sample, the cloth is bound completely, excluding nearly all the dye. The cord is tied at the bottom of the pouch of fabric, one end laid along the fabric pouch and the remainder of the cord lashed closely around until the top is reached and the two ends secured to each other.

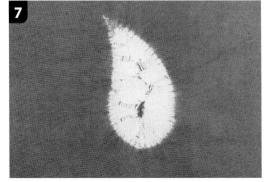

The pattern made by totally wrapping the cloth with your binding thread is nearly white. But note there is the small amount of dye that catches the unbound top, and the smallest amounts of dye that penetrate between the threads, creating very subtle texture.

different types of thread. We can use a thin polyester sewing thread or a chunkier string; this alters the amount of dye that penetrates the design.

Each variation is clearly explained in the images of the paisley pattern.

Using Two Rows of Stitching

Further possibilities are achieved by sewing a second row of stitches within your first shape, and binding just the central segment. The central segment can be bound in any of the three ways outlined above.

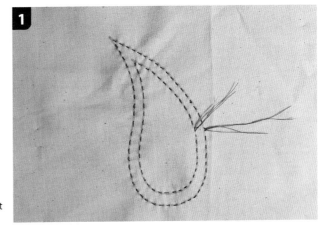

We have exactly the same paisley shape, but in this example, two lines of stitching are made, one 5mm (³/₁₆in) inside the other. The idea is to create a darker outline around the bound shape, adding yet another distinctive design possibility.

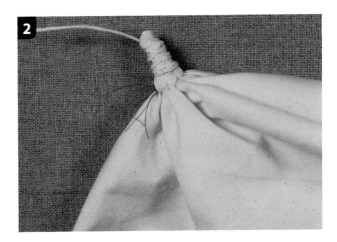

The gathered cloth is bound with a thick thread, but only the inner stitched area, leaving an unbound area of fabric between the two lines of stitching. Additionally, this same design could be bound with a thin polyester thread or totally wrapped, giving further options.

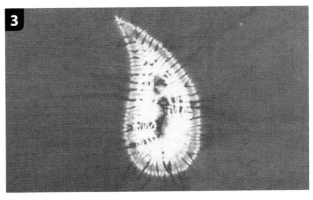

The design is achieved by just binding the inner stitched area, giving a darker outline to the whole shape. The outer line of stitching is quite distinct against the much whiter centre. This way of working produces a halo effect.

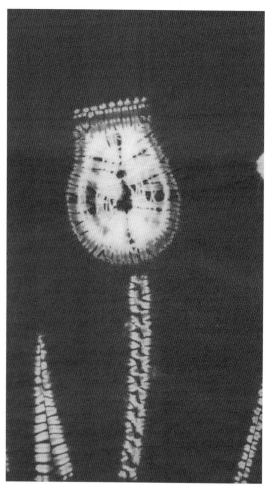

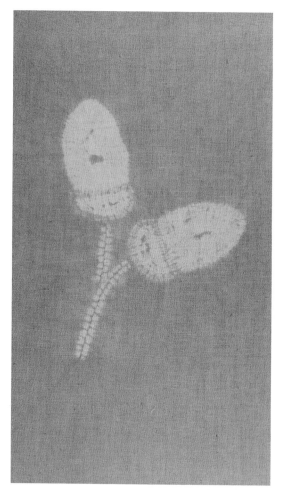

A simple seedhead using the technique of making two lines of stitching, inner and outer, then only binding the inner stitched area. The halo effect here helps give the impression of a hairy or fibrous shell to the seedhead.

This motif of acorns and cups is formed by combining two ways of binding. The cups are made by two rounds of stitching and binding the centre only. The acorns, which are smoother, are created by binding the gathered shape completely, excluding nearly all the dye.

Using two rows of stitching gives the effect of a halo, suggesting the faint edge of a dandelion clock or a downy seedhead. The two ways of working can be used together to good effect, as in the acorn motif. The cup is stitched with two rows of stitches to give the impression of the rough woody edge, and the acorn itself is smoother and therefore created with one row of stitching and closely bound.

Step-by-Step Maki-Age Technique

The outline of the shape is sewn with a double thread, leaving the ends free. The free ends are then pulled up tightly, creating a pouch of fabric, finishing with a knot to secure the shape. The thinner stitching thread can be used to bind the pouch of fabric. I prefer to use a fingering or double-knit weight thread. Begin by tying a knot at the base of the shape and work up the

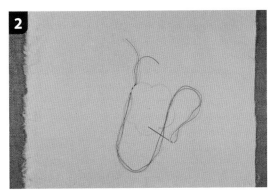

Let us take this effective and simple design shape of a five-petalled flower and learn step by step how to create with maki-age, looking closely at the stitching and binding technique.

The design outline is drawn on the fabric. As a guide, the design shown here is 6cm (2³/₈in) across. Prepare a double thread, no tag is needed, just leave a long end of thread. Stitch along the outline.

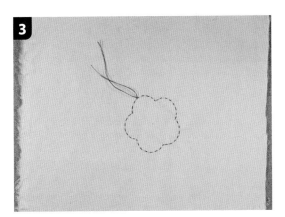

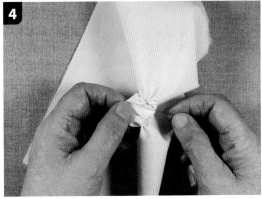

Keep the stitch sizes small and neat, a length of 2–3mm (¹/₁₆–¹/₈in) when sewing maki-age, this ensures the fabric can be evenly and closely gathered. Always have the start and finish stitching at an outer edge of the shape. Follow the outline accurately.

Hold the centre of the shape and pull on both of the threads. This is where the small stitches used ensure an even gathering of the fabric.

Once the two threads have been pulled up as tightly as possible, secure the gathering by tying a reef knot. This holds the gathered pouch of fabric in place for binding.

Cut a piece of binding thread, approximately 30cm (12in) long. Place the pouch of fabric in the centre of the binding thread as both ends of the thread will be used in a crisscross manner up the fabric.

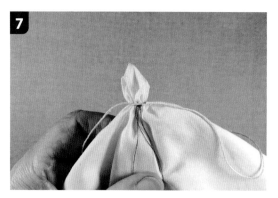

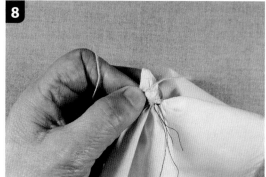

Secure the binding thread at the base of the gathered pouch with a knot. Make certain the thread securely covers the outline stitching thread, to assist in excluding the dye.

Keep the thread tight as you bind. Crisscross the thread, round and round the gathered fabric, until it is all wrapped.

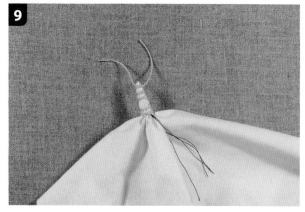

Here the cloth is completely bound. Make the last binding as near to the top as you are able. Finish by tying a knot in the two wrapped threads, and it is ready for dyeing.

gathered fabric, crisscrossing the thread until the top is reached, and then tie the ends together.

SEGMENTED DESIGNS

If you want to create a design where the shape may be tricky to bind in one, simply divide the shape and bind two smaller areas. The waning moon design is an instance of this approach to stitching maki-age.

It is helpful when sewing many segments to always start stitching on the outside of the overall design. This provides much better access to threads when pulling and binding.

Another striking use of the technique is when you want to produce a lot of irregular texture on a shape. This can be achieved by dividing the shape up into segments. Each small piece can then be stitched and bound separately. This can be an intricate and involved process and calls for dexterous fingers.

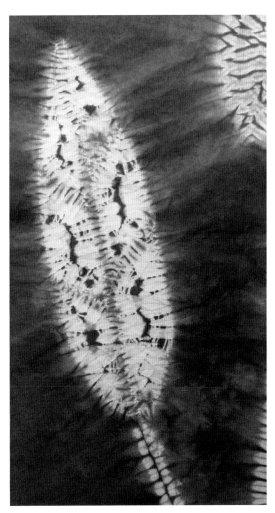

A waning moon created with maki-age shibori. The moon outline has been divided into two sections. It is an elongated shape and trying to completely exclude the dye in a long shape can be a challenge, so it is better to divide into segments on a longer shape.

This seedhead, 17cm (6½in) long, was created from six small sections of maki-age shibori. In this design, dividing it into segments was deliberately used to create lots of texture.

Step-by-Step Poppy Seedhead

The poppy seed design describes step by step the organisation of stitching required for a successful outcome when creating a design using various segments. With a design similar to this, the divisions can be arbitrary, but will be more effective if the sections reflect the structure of the plant or creature being portrayed.

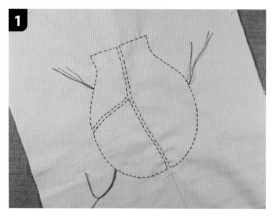

For a larger design, split the shape into sections, using the divisions to suggest texture. Additionally, the natural segments of the seedhead can hint at where to divide the motif. Note that the stitching rows are always started on outside of each shape.

Gather up each area of stitched outlines and tie firmly. Trim the long ends of threads to a length easier to knot together. At this stage, it is clear why it is best to always start the stitching on the outside of the segments.

To bind each pouch in turn, secure the binding thread closely around the stitching line. At this point be as accurate as you can. The binding is made by crisscrossing the thread until the top of each shape is reached. Make a knot at the top.

The stem of the poppy seedhead is made by using ori-nui stitch, but here use two rows of stitch parallel to each other to create a more substantial line.

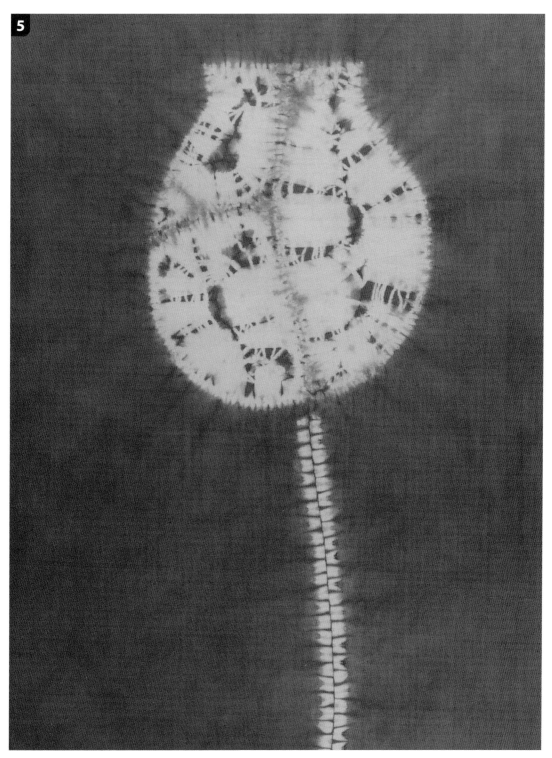

5

The completed poppy seedhead is 13.5cm (5³/₈in) high. The pink is created with madder root dye. The bindings give much surface texture and interest to the final design.

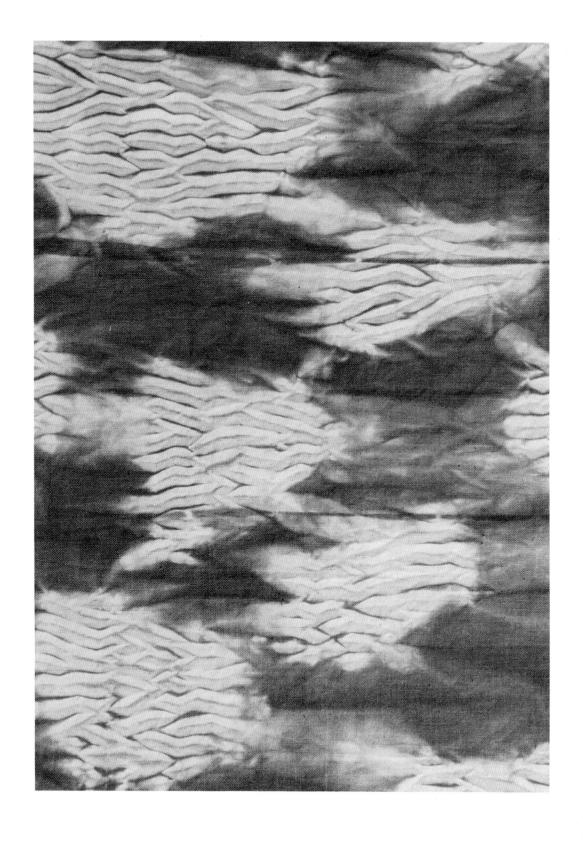

CHAPTER 8

MOKUME SHIBORI

Mokume shibori is one of the most pleasing and attractive shibori stitch designs, but also the most time consuming. Choose carefully if you want to use its distinctive texture, as you are committing to lots of sewing.

This stitch is particularly time consuming because it is sewn through just one layer of fabric. This technique consists of many parallel rows of stitching close together. The pattern creates an overall texture suggesting woodgrain or water ripples. When stitched successfully with the correct spacing, practically all evidence of the stitching lines disappears in the finished cloth.

We will consider the simple but time-rich process of creating mokume stitch and some variations, which create a different rhythm across the cloth. Varying the relationship of stitches in the parallel rows alters the pattern achieved.

The stitch can also be formed in short, small blocks by using floating threads between blocks of stitch. And in this way, mokume can be successfully worked around a shape, leaving a coloured area sitting in the middle of the texture. The floating threads are kept to the back of the fabric, allowing the unstitched areas to hold the dye.

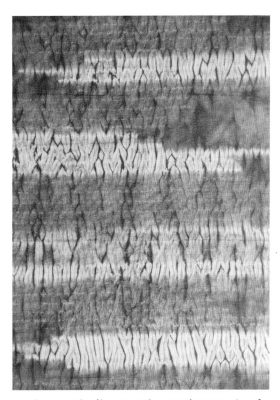

Another example of how to easily create the suggestion of water. This piece was stitched all over, dyed once, then some rows of stitching removed (the shadow of some stitching can be seen), and then dyed again, giving the effect of light on water.

◀ A watery design, typical of the pattern produced from mokume shibori, a subtle flowing texture.

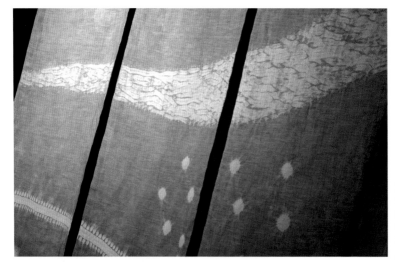

Mokume can be successfully used in shibori landscapes to suggest a swath of a crop or a field. This was worked on a heavy linen so the resulting texture is bolder. (Photo: Daniel Rushall)

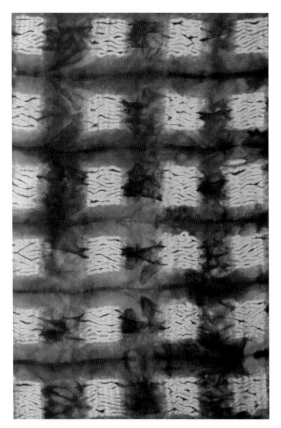

This is an example of shibori weaving. First, work a small block of mokume stitching, and then take the thread behind the fabric. Bring the needle up and stitch another block. This is continued across the fabric. This is stitched on silk, which results in a finer texture.

And the reverse of that is to create a textured design motif in the centre of the plain dyed fabric. When forming a central motif, the rows of stitching need to be close together. Preferably the rows are made 5mm (³/₁₆in) apart to maintain the mokume effect over a small design.

THE PROCESS OF MOKUME STITCH

To begin, draw a grid of lines 6mm (¹/₄in) apart on a sheet of A3 or A4 paper. If you are truly inspired by this technique, make another sheet with lines 5mm (³/₁₆in) apart. Make the drawn lines a dark colour, and you will be able to see through your fabric to transfer the lines whenever you want to sew mokume.

We will look at two samples, one where the placing of the stitching is staggered, and the other where the stitches all line up. In both these samples, I used a piece of fabric 20cm (8in) square and ruled lines every 6mm (¹/₄in).

When pulling up the rows of stitching, it is most important to be sure that all the rows are pulled up equally, and gathered back to the very beginning of each row. This attention to detail at this point ensures a good result. Next, row by row, give a final pull and tie a tag into the end of each row of stitches. Work methodically down the fabric to be certain that you do not miss a row.

Another tip is to look at the back of the fabric while pulling the threads, and you will be able to see clearly how well you have gathered it.

Staggered Stitch Rows

As usual, using a double thread with a tag in the end, stitch along the marked line. The stitch lengths should be varied. On the following row the stitches are staggered in relation to the previous row's stitches. This is how the beautiful meandering pattern is created.

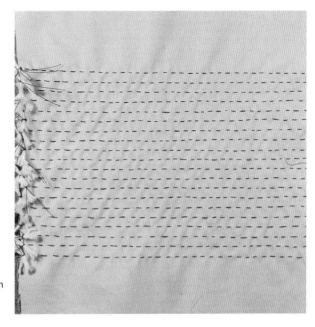

This is the stitching for mokume. The stitching is made in rows 6mm (¹⁄₄in) apart. Mark up your fabric in parallel rows. Each length of stitch is varied, between 3–6mm (¹⁄₈–¹⁄₄in) long.

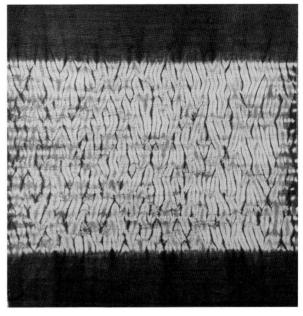

This is a classic mokume or wood grain pattern. The cloth folds itself around the irregular stitches, producing this flowing design. Note that the direction of the resulting pattern is at 90° to that of the stitching.

It is important to note that the pattern is created at right angles to the stitching lines. Carefully think about the required direction of the finished design, before beginning.

In-Line Stitch Rows

The needle, thread and tag used are exactly the same as above, but in this case the individual stitches in each row are all in line with each other. This way of stitching creates a pattern of white lines. Sew an even number of stitches in each row, so that the thread starts and finishes on the same side of the fabric.

These stitches are best used tapered in recreating natural structures. Mark the lines carefully to be certain the rows taper evenly.

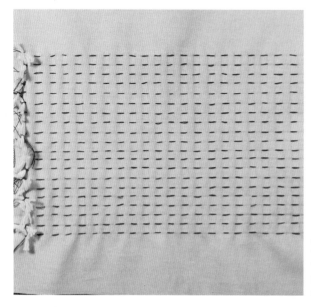

Again, the rows are 6mm (¹/₄ in) apart. In contrast, here the stitches in each of the rows line up with those in the preceding row. It is helpful to rule further lines at right angles to ensure even stitches. Stitch length is 4mm (³/₁₆in).

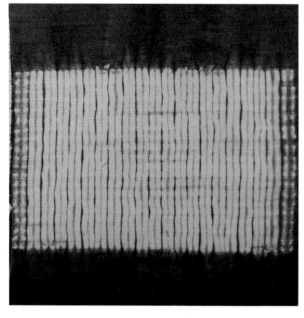

Here is the resulting pattern from regular size stitches, all in line with each other. This pattern can be tapered, with stitches in line but increasing in size, thereby creating a downy thistle head or eucalyptus flower.

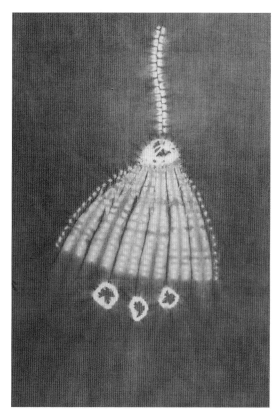

A small hanging flower head to illustrate the effect achieved when the in-line mokume stitch is tapered. The cloth needs to be marked clearly and carefully to ensure even tapering of rows to achieve the desired effect.

This stitch makes wonderful thistle tops, eucalyptus flowers and delicate hanging forms, as illustrated.

Troubleshooting

One of the common mistakes with mokume is to stitch the lines too far apart, resulting in the stitched lines being visible and the woodgrain pattern is not achieved. In addition, the balance of thread to weight of fabric is also important. Look at my green oak leaf design and see how visible the lines are. Only after my disappointment on unpicking it, did I remember that I used a heavier weight polyester thread. That tiny difference in thickness meant the folds did not gather well and my stitching lines show. Careful attention to every detail pays off.

The indigo oak leaf overleaf illustrates how the pattern should look. The lines of stitching are barely visible and the mokume pattern flows up the leaf, suggesting the leaf veins.

Before starting on a planned design, it will be worthwhile making a small sample. Use your chosen fabric and the preferred distance between rows to ensure you can achieve the effect you want. This time spent at the beginning of a mokume project will pay dividends.

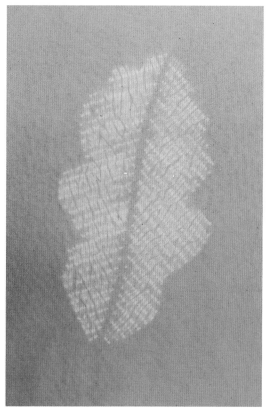

This oak leaf motif is to illustrate how not to do mokume. The line of the stitches overwhelms the finished pattern, and the flow of the design is interrupted by these visible lines. In this case, the thread was too thick for the fabric.

This oak leaf is successful; there are hints of the stitch lines, but the flowing pattern predominates. Always test thread and fabric before commencing a big project.

CREATIVE VARIATIONS WITH MOKUME TECHNIQUE

The Spaced/Woven Pattern

Simple geometric designs can be formed by using small blocks of stitch spaced out with unstitched areas alternating between. The pattern needs to be carefully measured and drawn onto the fabric. The long threads linking the small areas of stitch should all run along the surface of the same side of the fabric. Start each row with double thread and a tag to secure the stitching. Additionally, each row in the small blocks of stitch needs to be staggered with the previous one. The shapes of the small blocks can be varied to build diverse designs.

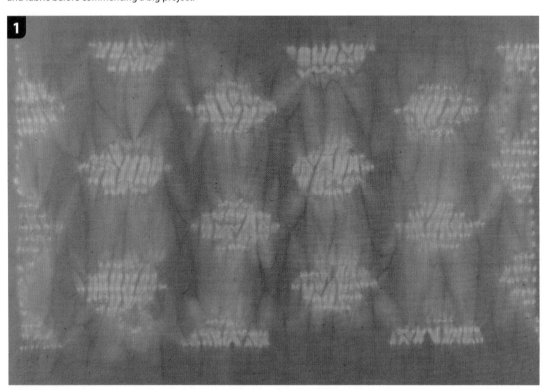

A simple geometric design is formed by using small blocks of stitch, spaced out with unstitched areas alternating between. The pattern needs to be carefully measured and drawn onto the fabric. The rows are 6mm (¹/₄in) apart.

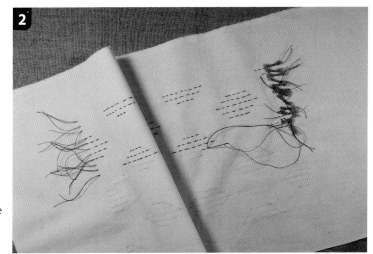

Start each row with double thread and a tag to secure the stitching. Each row in the small blocks of stitch needs to be staggered with the previous one. Take the thread behind the fabric and bring the needle up at the next block.

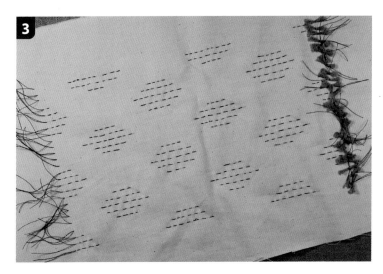

The front side after all the stitching is completed. These small lozenges are 5.5 × 2.4cm (2¼ × 1in). Each row of lozenges is spaced one row below the previous row to allow the dye to penetrate the plain areas of cloth.

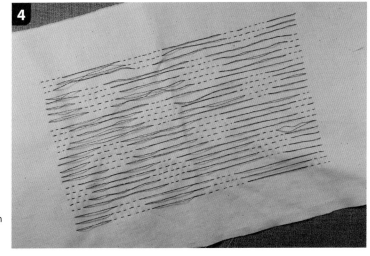

The back side of the fabric all completed, showing how the threads run between the mokume blocks of stitch. Care has to be taken not to catch the thread of the adjacent row. Turn and check regularly as you proceed.

Working Mokume Around Shapes

One of the most pleasing but also the most time-consuming ways of using mokume is to place a motif within a sea of stitching. Many rows of stitching are necessary to create a design in a field of mokume stitch.

This is illustrated here by the bird skimming across the sky and lily pads floating in a pond. There are many possible design ideas that can be created. The kind of motifs used need to be simple in outline, as there will be some blurring around the edges of the shapes.

The effect created is delicate and ethereal. As a reminder, if setting out on a project like this, do a sample piece first on your chosen fabric to ensure a successful outcome.

The complete lily pad design. Note how the leaf shapes are slightly broken into by the background texture. This will occur and the reason it is best to keep to simple shapes. The mokume pattern flows at right angles to the rows of stitching.

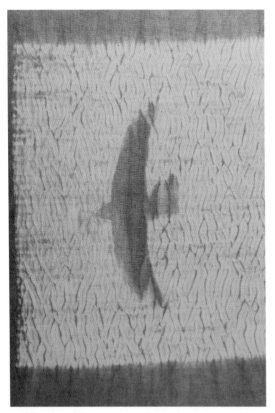

A flying bird against a sky of mokume rows. The shape is elongated, and some sharpness has been lost on the tips of the wings and head. But to me the overall impression is of the hazy sky on a summer day.

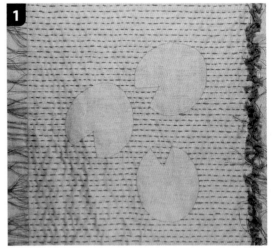

The outline of the leaves is drawn clearly to enable accurate stopping and starting of stitching. Here the lines are sewn 6mm (1/4in) apart, and all the stitches are staggered in relation to the adjacent row.

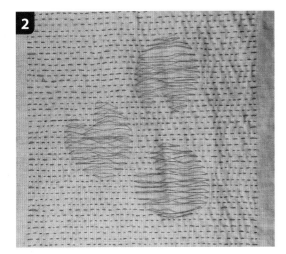

The reverse shows how the rows of stitching skip across the back of the fabric where the shapes are placed. It is important to make sure the threads do not get twisted on the reverse of the cloth.

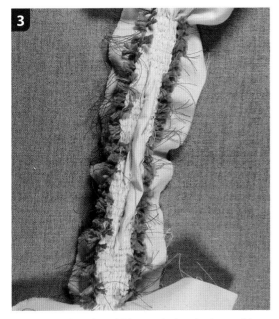

The completely gathered fabric, with the raised area of the cloth protruding from the areas of background stitching. Thereby these areas of the unstitched pattern catch the dye and form the design.

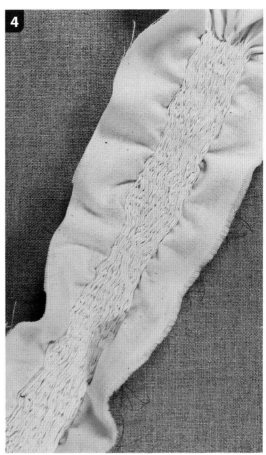

The reverse of the gathered cloth. To look at the back of the mokume gathers is a useful way of checking that all the stitching is pulled up as tightly as possible.

Working Mokume Within Shapes

Likewise, mokume is excellent for creating irregular shapes covered in its distinctive texture. The direction of the resulting pattern (at right angles to the rows of stitching) can be utilised successfully to suggest leaf veining, the texture of seedheads or grasses.

The challenge when creating a small shape is to maintain the integrity of the pattern,

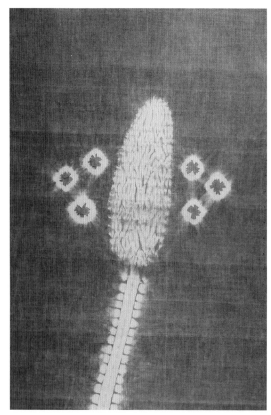

A plantain head created with mokume stitch. The design is a regular shape, it could be stitched in miru shibori but the choice to use this stitch instead, creates more texture in the final pattern. The plantain head is 17cm (6 ½in) in length.

Three odd shapes, making up a grass motif, most suitable for creating in mokume stitch. The cotton is a heavier weight and rows are correspondingly a little further apart at 1cm (³/₈in). As a guide, the upper triangular segment is 20cm (8in) long.

particularly where the motif narrows. When working the stitch in these designs, space the rows 5mm (³/₁₆in) apart.

How to Create a Pear

Let us look at creating a pear using mokume stitch, a simple but irregular motif, ideal for showing step-by-step mokume stitch within an outline. Draw a sharp and clear outline to guide the stitching. The pear measures 13.5cm (5¼in) from top to bottom. The rows are 5mm (³/₁₆in) apart.

Each row of stitching needs to start and finish exactly on the outer edges of the shape. Use small stitches for the short top and bottom rows to maintain the mokume effect. A little ori-nui stalk and leaf are added to complete the design.

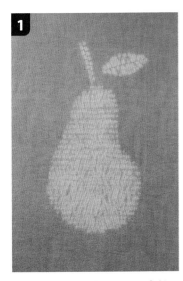

1

A simple but irregular pear motif, this is perfect for showing step by step how to work mokume stitch within an outline. Draw a sharp and clear outline to guide the stitching.

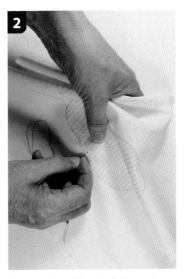

2

Draw a series of lines to follow at 5mm (³/₁₆in) apart. Always have the start and finish stitching at an outer edge of the shape. Enter the needle at the edge of the shape, carefully following the line.

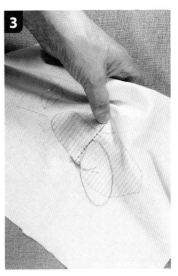

3

One row is completed; bring the needle to finish exactly on the outline of the pear motif. Trim the thread. Execute each following row in exactly the same way.

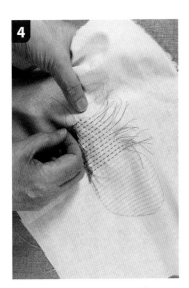

4

Half the pear is sewn. Stagger the stitches in each parallel row as much as possible to ensure the flowing mokume pattern is achieved.

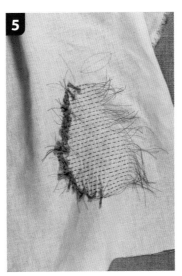

5

The mokume stitching now completely covers the pear. Take extra care stitching the short top and bottom rows. Use small stitches for these rows to maintain the mokume effect.

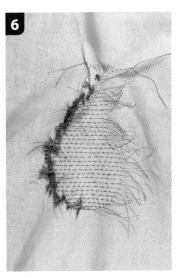

6

A short stem and leaf are added in ori-nui stitch to complete the design. The fabric is ready for gathering and then dyeing.

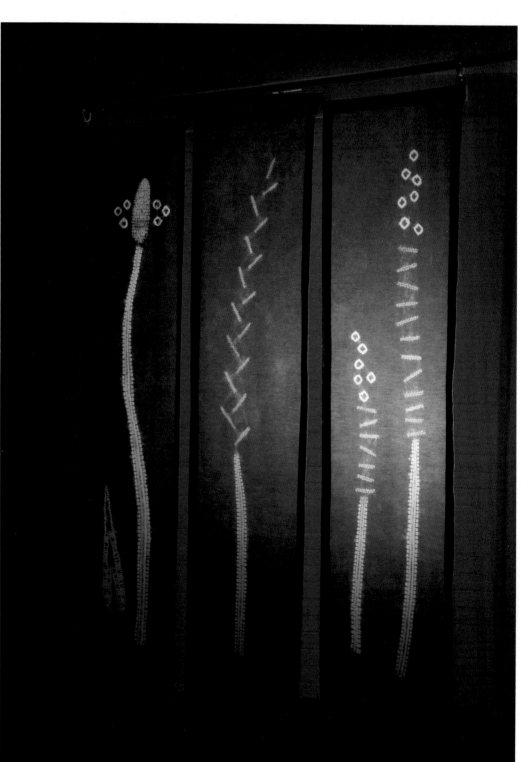

CHAPTER 9

PUTTING IT ALL TOGETHER

Though beautiful in their own right, each shibori pattern we have explored in the previous chapters can be combined to create more wonderful shibori creations. In previous chapters, particularly on miru and maki-age shibori, I have used short lengths of ori-nui to enhance the designs. We are now going to explore more elaborate combinations of techniques. This will guide and encourage you to explore creating your own multi-technique patterns.

I will be suggesting various blends of stitches and also giving guidance on the best order of working and gathering when using different stitches. It is time well spent to stop and consider how to approach the sewing before launching into the work. As a guiding principle, give thought to how your fingers will be able to access all those intricate rows of stitches.

GENERAL GUIDELINES

There are useful pointers to help get the best results when using multiple types of stitches together. Over time I have found these simple rules and principles of working have always achieved a good outcome. The first step is always to draw your proposed design onto paper with all the lines and shapes clearly marked. Then transfer to the fabric ready for sewing.

This example of a straightforward composition of basic stitches builds up a whole garden border using just ori-nui, maki-age and some small boshi shapes. Curving the stems suggests movement and brings the design alive. The small boshi shapes created by tying a bead in and wrapping in plastic further reinforce the feeling of movement.

◄ Here is a series of three panels using five diverse shibori techniques. This shows how the various stitches can be combined to create a bold design. Each panel is 35 × 150cm (13³/₄ × 59in). (Photo: Daniel Rushall)

KEY POINTS WHEN STITCHING MULTIPLE TECHNIQUES

- Choose different colour threads when working a complex design to identify the various elements.
- Use masking tape to hold groups of thread when sewing.
- If beads are being used in a design, they must always be added first, attached with a small stitch to the reverse of the fabric in the position you want them, but not bound until the very end.
- When planning and spacing out beads, always leave a little more space than you think necessary. The binding of a bead takes more cloth than expected.
- Look at your overall arrangement of shapes and plan the direction of stitching. Always be methodical, keeping all the stitching in one direction. Start the threads at one edge of the cloth, working the stitches to the other end.

- Work across the fabric from left to right or top to bottom when sewing. If multiple small shapes are involved in an intricate design, it can be easy to miss a small essential stitch detail. I have done it!
- First stitch the techniques which are 'flat', maki-age outline stitches, mokume, and all those stitches which do not pucker or alter the fabric's profile.
- Next stitches would be those worked on the fold, miru, ori-nui and awase ori-nui. When using miru shibori as part of a pattern, in nearly all cases, stitch this before ori-nui to ensure the two sides of the pattern can be folded accurately.
- Any stitching of design elements using guntai shibori need to be done last, as this stitch distorts the cloth.

KEY POINTS FOR GATHERING MULTIPLE TECHNIQUES

- The first step is to bind the beads in. If left to later, it will be tricky to manipulate the cloth. Take care not to catch the dangling threads in the binding yarn.
- Binding of maki-age and boshi shapes is the next step to take, while the fabric is not too gathered.
- Look at the overall lines of stitching and plan the order of gathering. Always be methodical, work across the fabric from left to right or top to bottom when gathering.

- Use masking tape to hold groups of thread ends out of the way while gathering.
- Before dyeing, manipulate the fabric and push to the front with your fingers the small pouches of fabric from the back to the front to enable the total piece to collect as much dye as possible. A chunky crochet hook or the end of an artist's paintbrush is very useful for this task.

INSPIRATIONAL IDEAS FOR MIXING TECHNIQUES

Simple Combinations with Ori-Nui

It is possible to build pleasing and remarkable arrangements from the most straightforward of the processes. Designs can be formed from just ori-nui with some beads added or contrasted with awase ori-nui. I love to use ne-maki to suggest seeds, grasses, texture in a landscape or stars. Ori-nui makes interesting textures when combined in short rows, parallel or at an angle.

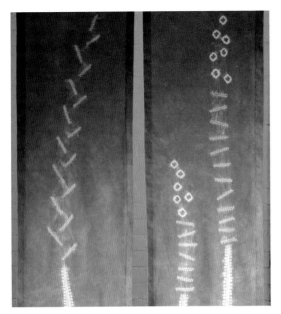

Simple ways of creating grass textures by utilising ne-maki, ori-nui and awase ori-nui. Short lengths of ori-nui either stacked on top of one another or placed at right angles can suggest particular grass types. The tied-in beads add more interest and bring to mind small seeds ready to be carried away on the wind. (Photo: Daniel Rushall)

In this example maki-nui and ori-nui lines are alternated, constructing a wave-like design with lots of interesting background texture from the closeness of the stitched lines. The beads break the rhythm and provide contrast.

One way of realising a landscape design in shibori. Plenty of repeated lines of ori-nui suggest a field of crops, small beads scattered to create distant texture and a strong bold line of awase ori-nui to define where the sky and land meet. A boshi shibori moon brings the design alive.

Additionally, ori-nui is always successful when placed alongside rows of maki-nui, hinting at a watery texture; and stunning borders of flowers are easy to accomplish with ori-nui plus a few maki-age shapes bound and tied for contrast.

Mainly Miru

Miru shibori has to be my most loved technique of them all. As a result, many of my multiple designs include some miru shibori. In these compositions, miru is the star of the show. It is most effectively used to build multiple leaf shapes along a branch. The motifs are positioned at different angles along a branch of awase ori-nui. For further interest, add maki-age or boshi shibori to hint at berries and seedheads.

Simple bold shapes like these vegetable examples are perfect to show miru at its very best. And by adding just a few tiny beads or some ori-nui leaves, the impression of a squash or a beetroot is made.

Several miru shibori leaves along a distinct stem of awase ori-nui. This is the type of design where awase ori-nui comes into its own as the prominent element holding the design together. To ensure the awase ori-nui line is consistent involves measuring, marking and creasing the cloth with care. Small maki-age berries complete the design with a topping of three lines of mokume.

A vivid squash shape in miru shibori stitched on a folded fabric. The small beads are attached to the back of the fabric before all the many rows of stitching are sewn. They are bound in once all the stitching is complete.

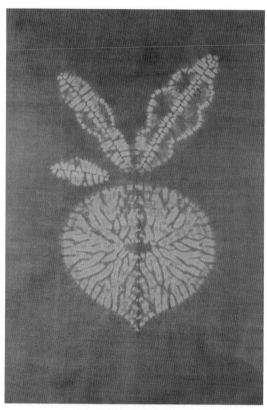

Miru shibori is contrasted here with the lightness of ori-nui stitched outlines. The design must be drawn flat with leaf details marked clearly. First, the three leaf shapes are stitched. Then the root shape is folded in two and sewn. This is sewn on a light fabric with 5mm ($^3/_{16}$in) between each row.

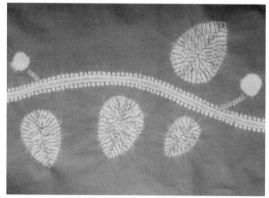

Miru shibori is used here with a pronounced awase ori-nui line to link all the segments of the design together. There are a multitude of possibilities with this design idea of miru leaves along a stem, as many as there are leaf shapes in nature.

Creating Flowers

I find great pleasure in designing flowers in shibori. The most appropriate stitches to form a flower head are miru, ori-nui and mokume. Miru can be used to make the cone or the main bract of a flower. Lines of ori-nui or blocks of mokume successfully create the petals and massed stamens and florets of particular species. For a bold stem, use awase ori-nui or that lovely combination of an inner line of maki-nui and an outer line of ori-nui.

This daisy flower head is also made from three stitches. The stem is formed from the interesting combination of maki-nui and ori-nui stitch. The cone of the flower is shaped with miru, as it creates a distinct and clear structure. Again ori-nui is used to make the more delicate petals.

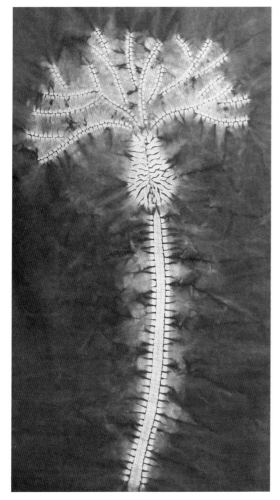

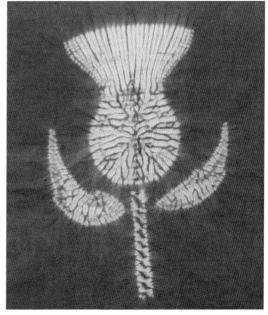

A knapweed flower is made from three stitches. The stem is formed from a line of prominent awase ori-nui. The bract is in miru shibori because it gives a bold strong shape and the lighter fronds of the flower head are worked in ori-nui, as it is a more delicate stitch.

This thistle head incorporates more shibori stitches. It is a good example of the use of two needles from one point to form odd shaped leaves; and coming out of the bold miru bract are the florets, constructed from many rows of in-line mokume.

MULTIPLE STITCH COMBINATIONS

Scattering simple shapes such as circles, squares or paisley over the cloth and using myriad shibori techniques is a great way to experiment with different stitches and their design outcomes. Such a pattern can become a sampler to assist in future projects.

To start with, such overall patterns help you to get a feel for what a stitch can suggest. The end result is also pleasing. Some time is needed to calculate what stitch will give the best effect for certain flowers, animals or shells. Look at

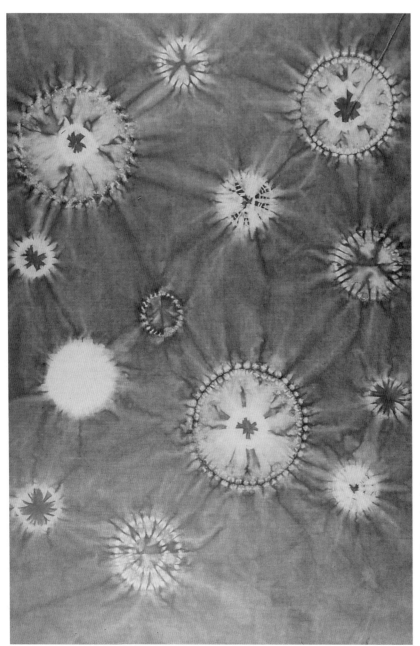

Another type of design to dream up with varied shibori stitches; a random scattering of shapes across the cloth formed from a great diversity of stitches. The bolder forms are stitched with an outer circle of ori-nui or maki-nui with a bead bound into the centre. It is a very simple construction but most attractive.

A leaping salmon, of which the principal stitch used, to realise the effect of scales, is mokume shibori. The other stitches are ori-nui to build the outline and create the tail and head, taking the stitching away from the fold. A bead for an eye brings the fish to life.

Multiple techniques are utilised in this bird and tree arrangement. Again, awase ori-nui forms the strong vertical element across the cloth. Small and bold miru leaves along with ne-maki beads create a background for the bird. Mokume, maki-age, ori-nui and maki-nui are employed to form the bird.

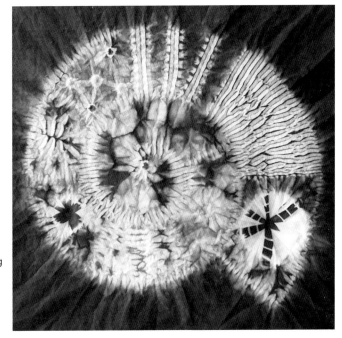

A wonderful sampler of many stitches creates an ammonite. Mokume texture, awase ori-nui lines, ne-maki bound beads, large and small, are all featured in this design. A simple running stitch through one layer is used to frame the design. Generally, a single line of stitch does not create a good resist, but when used as an outline to a complicated pattern, it will be effective, as here.

the fish as an example of how to select stitches. Mokume is just perfect for scales on the back. The clear outline needs ori-nui and the tail and head need a bolder line and two rows of stitching on the fold create this; and of course, a tiny bead for the eye.

After all this time of practice, I still have to make a couple of attempts to create a complex design in shibori. Be willing to experiment and make mistakes. We learn so much from our errors.

A Multi-Technique Project: A Vase of Flowers

This vase design uses most of the shibori techniques and clearly shows the recommended order of working a complicated design. Read each caption along with the key points for sewing multiple techniques earlier in this chapter. This will give you useful guidance on creating your own multiple patterns. As a size guide, the vase is 11cm (4¹/₂in) across the base and 27cm (11in) high overall.

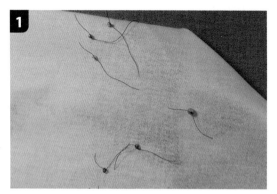

The first step is to fix the beads, attach with a small stitch to the reverse of the fabric in the position you want them. Always leave a little more space than you think necessary when planning and spacing out beads. The binding of a bead takes more cloth than expected.

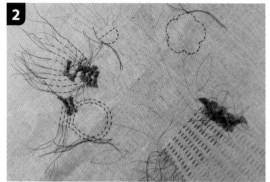

Look at your overall arrangement of shapes and first select and stitch all the techniques which are 'flat'; maki-age outline stitches, mokume, any stitching with two needles from one point; simply put, all those stitches which do not pucker or alter the fabrics profile. Ensure you keep all stitching ends to the outside of the design to allow it to be easily accessible at the gathering stage.

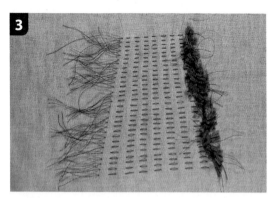

A close-up detail of the stitching required to form the vase, in-line mokume stitching. Carefully rule a grid to assist in keeping the stitching as regular as possible. The stitches taper from bottom to top to give an overall striped effect.

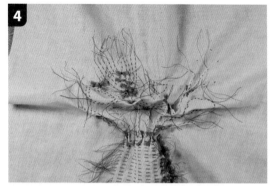

Next stitches would be those worked on the fold, miru, ori-nui and awase ori-nui. When using miru shibori as part of a pattern, in nearly all cases, stitch this before ori-nui to ensure the two sides of the pattern can be folded accurately. Additionally, think carefully about the direction of stitching. Start all the rows at the top of the vase and work outwards and upwards.

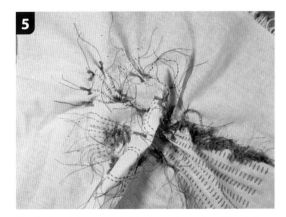

The final technique to stitch is those elements of the design that are formed from guntai shibori. Here we have a four-petalled flower and the jug handle and spout. This is the last stitching to carry out, as it tends to distort the cloth.

The completed and gathered cloth; always plan the order of gathering. Be methodical, work across the fabric from left to right or top to bottom when gathering. If small pouches of fabric have gathered at the back of the work, manipulate these and push to the front to enable the total piece to collect as much dye as possible.

The completed vase created with multiple techniques. When working with a piece so densely gathered, it is necessary to carefully agitate and manipulate the fabric in the dye bath. This is to ensure that the dye gets into all the in-between spaces. But do come to accept any small mistakes or not-quite-perfect results and enjoy the overall result!

FURTHER INFORMATION

UK

The Hemp Shop
THS Ltd, Tirelands Farm, Tirelands Lane,
Enmore, Bridgwater, Somerset TA5 2DR
www.thehempshop.co.uk
A range of hemp and organic fabrics. The fabric
mainly used to create the samples in this book is
Classic Hemp Cloth.

Whaleys Bradford Ltd
Harris Court, Great Horton, Bradford, West
Yorkshire BD7 4EQ
www.whaleys-bradford.ltd.uk
Long established fabric merchant. A recommended
cloth for shibori is Calico AJ404 Scoured Natural.

Wild Colours
Studio 319, Scott House, The Custard
Factory, Gibb Street, Deritend,
Birmingham B9 4DT
www.wildcolours.co.uk
A great range of natural dyes and assistants
plus a selection of dye extracts for ease and
quickness of use.

Sew Essential Ltd
Unit 4, Marquis Court, Marquis Drive Moira,
Swadlincote, Derbyshire DE12 6EJ
www.sewessential.co.uk
General haberdashery, fabric marker pens and
Gutermann threads.

George Weil & Sons Ltd
Old Portsmouth Road, Peasmarsh,
Guildford GU13 1LZ
www.georgeweil.com
General craft supplies; natural dyes, Procion dyes,
and strong binding threads.

Empress Mills
Glyde Works, Byron Road, Colne,
Lancashire BB8 0BQ
www.empressmills.co.uk
A large range of haberdashery and general sewing
equipment.

USA & CANADA

Dharma Trading Co
1604 4th Street, San Rafael, CA 94901
www.dharmatrading.com
Supplier of fibre reactive dyes, a range of cotton
fabrics and cotton and silk clothes blanks. Note
calico is called muslin in the USA and Canada.

Maiwa
1663 Duranleau St, Vancouver, BC V6H 3S3
www.maiwa.com
Suppliers of dyeable fabrics and clothes blanks for
dyeing and natural dyes and assistants.
Botanical Colors
4020 Leary Way, Ste 300, Seattle WA 98107
www.botanicalcolors.com
Specialist in natural dyes.

Rit Dyes
www.ritdye.com
Suppliers of Rit dyes and a great selection of colour
formulas to create your own shades.

Pro Chemical & Dye
126 Shove Street, Fall River, MA 02724
https://prochemicalanddye.net/
Suppliers of Procion and other chemical dyes plus
fabrics for dyeing.

FURTHER READING AND INSPIRATION

*Shibori: The Inventive Art of Japanese Shaped
Resist Dyeing by Yoshiko Iwamoto, Mary Kellogg
Rice and Jane Barton (Kodansha USA, 2012)
Stitched Shibori by Jane Callender (Search
Press, 2017)
Shibori for Textile Artists by Janice Gunner
(Batsford, 2018)
Colours From Nature by Jenny Dean (Search
Press, 2009)
Botany for the Artist by Sarah Simblet (DK, 2020)*

INDEX

First published in 2024 by
The Crowood Press Ltd
Ramsbury, Marlborough
Wiltshire SN8 2HR

enquiries@crowood.com
www.crowood.com

British Library Cataloguing-in-Publication Data
A catalogue record for this book is available from the British Library.

ISBN 978 0 7198 4349 5

Cover design by Sergey Tsvetkov

All photographs are the author's own except where otherwise credited.

Typeset by Envisage IT
Printed and bound in India by Replika Press Pvt. Ltd.

DEDICATION

To my husband Alf, known to many as John, for all the creative support and encouragement he has given me throughout our many years together.

ACKNOWLEDGEMENTS

It has been an incredible opportunity to be asked to write this book on shibori, a challenge that I took on without knowing about the extensive commitment needed for such an endeavour. A big thanks to all those other creative book writers who have said just the right thing at the right time or been there when I needed them to be: Jen Goodwin, Sarah Morrish, Kyleigh Orlebar and Amber Hards. To the Sherborne Netwalk group whose unwavering support and interest in the progress of the book have been a constant source of motivation.

And finally, my deepest gratitude to all those who have attended my workshops over the years. Your enthusiasm and talent in creating beautiful fabrics have not only inspired me, but have also fed my creativity, sparking new thoughts, ideas and directions. A few of the pieces shown in the book were produced on my shibori workshops. While the passage of time means some names are now forgotten, I am very grateful for your creative contributions.